"Surprisingly moving. Her sincerity and intensity of feeling are re-markably, palpably real. As she becomes more loving, forgiving, more grateful, more aware of her own blessings, it is impossible not to feel the same." —*The Boston Globe*

"Tender and funny . . . reverent and ribald, harried and hopeful . . . a witty memoir of a troubled soul grappling with her failings and the deepest mysteries of salvation." —*The Denver Sunday Post*

"Candid, entertaining, and abundantly enlightening, *Looking for Mary* sizzles with the fervor of the seeker and the sought-after, and delivers between its covers a sweet and salty miracle." —*Elle*

"This chronicle does not read like an exercise in wish-fulfillment. It feels rather like the story of a woman who, after decades of seek-ing, found her mother, and through her, discovered herself." —*Publishers Weekly* (starred review)

"An incredibly honest account of one daughter-mother trying to make sense of the roles she has been given, the mistakes she has made, the heartaches she has felt." —*The Anniston Star*

"A tale of adventure, both outwardly, into the world, and inwardly, into the soul." —*Boston Herald*

"A full-bodied portrait of her inner struggle to achieve grace." —*Booklist*

"Deeply personal and wonderfully written, this book invites the reader to confront skeptical attitudes about religion, religious prac-tices, and religious dogmas and step into the divine light." —*Library Journal*

"An irreverent, laugh-out-loud conversion story . . . quirky, con-vincing, and ultimately very moving." —*Ft. Worth Morning Star-Telegram*

PENGUIN COMPASS

LOOKING FOR MARY

Beverly Donofrio's first book, *Riding in Cars with Boys,* became a cult classic and is now a feature film produced by James L. Brooks, directed by Penny Marshall, and starring Drew Barrymore. *Looking for Mary* began as a radio documentary for National Public Radio. Donofrio currently lives in Mexico.

PENGUIN COMPASS

BEVERLY DONOFRIO

Looking for
Mary

OR,

THE

BLESSED MOTHER

AND ME

PENGUIN COMPASS

PENGUIN BOOKS
Published by the Penguin Group
Penguin Group (USA) Inc., 375 Hudson Street, New York, New York 10014, U.S.A.
Penguin Books Ltd, 80 Strand, London WC2R 0RL, England
Penguin Books Australia Ltd, 250 Camberwell Road, Camberwell, Victoria 3124, Australia
Penguin Books Canada Ltd, 10 Alcorn Avenue, Toronto, Ontario, Canada M4V 3B2
Penguin Books India (P) Ltd, 11 Community Centre, Panchsheel Park, New Delhi – 110 017, India
Penguin Books (N.Z.) Ltd, Cnr Rosedale and Airborne Roads, Albany, Auckland, New Zealand
Penguin Books (South Africa) (Pty) Ltd, 24 Sturdee Avenue,
Rosebank, Johannesburg 2196, South Africa

Penguin Books Ltd, Registered Offices: 80 Strand, London WC2R 0RL, England

First published in the United States of America by
Viking Compass, a member of Penguin Putnam Inc., 2000
Published in Penguin Compass 2001

9   10

Copyright © Beverly Donofrio, 2000
All rights reserved

Illustrations by Jorge Alberto Asato Espana

THE LIBRARY OF CONGRESS HAS CATALOGED
THE HARDCOVER EDITION AS FOLLOWS:
Donofrio, Beverly.
Looking for Mary, or, The Blessed Mother and me/
Beverly Donofrio.
p.   cm.
ISBN 0-670-88459-6 (hc.)
ISBN 0 14 01.9627 7 (pbk)
1. Donofrio, Beverly   2. Mary, Blessed Virgin, Saint.
I. Title: Blessed Mother and me.   II. Title.
BX4705.D6146 A3   2000
282'.092—dc21
[B]
00–036790

Printed in the United States of America
Set in Adobe Garamond
Designed by Francesca Belanger

This book is for Mary.

And for my parents, Louise and
Edward Donofrio.

Acknowledgments

This book was read by many people at different stages. Everyone offered invaluable encouragement and suggestions that influenced the final book. To all of you—Tony Cohan, Kristen Dehner, Trudy Dittmar, Jay Derrah, Robin Tewes, Jason Budrow, Denise Sirkot, Beatriz Bell, Ana Theil, Sue McKinney Ortega, Karen Gadbois, Tony Connor, Gina Hyams, Angela Matano, Linda Garrett, Paige Evans, Elizabeth Levy, Julie Rigby, Georgian Lussier, Mark Jacobson, Barbara Cavanagh, Heather Woodbury, Susan O'Meara, Jackie Austin, Julie Ansel—I am deeply grateful.

I thank Jorge Alberto Asato Espana for his inspired illustrations.

By being open to my idea to go looking for Mary four years ago, and by coaxing from me what I really felt about the Virgin Mary, David Isay changed my life. And Stacy Abrahamson helped him do it.

Nancy Sawastynowicz cleaned my house, taught me to garden and gather seaweed and scallops and clams from the bay. Nancy Sawastynowicz loved me so much she turned my heart around.

. . .

I must thank Jacki Lyden for dragging me to Ireland, and Amy Marcus for helping me drag Jacki to Knock; Alex Kotlowitz walked with me through the wax museum in Fatima; and Masako Takahashi helped me find "The Night That Never Sleeps," a sublime Assumption of the Virgin fiesta in a tiny Mexican town.

Renee Montagne gave me a warm home and friendship in LA, and Jim Brooks gave me an office with a view and a couch, and his reassuring laugh booming down the hall.

Father Slavko Barbaric was an inspiration, and Father Bill Kiel a comfort.

If Gail Hochman, my agent and angel, hadn't been so loyal and indomitable, and taken by my Mary collection in Orient; if my first editor at Viking, Mindy Werner, hadn't had faith in me; if my "special" editor, Beena Kamlani, hadn't been so brilliant, insightful, and gently forthright; if my editor, Pam Dorman, hadn't been so tireless and insistent; and if Susan Hans O'Connor hadn't kept on top of things, this book might have been called *Hearts and Daggers* and never made it to print.

Without my son, Jason, I would not be so rich and would have much less to share. And without my parents' love and humor, their support and their good hearts, I would not have had the courage to write anything at all.

Looking for Mary

OR,

THE BLESSED MOTHER
AND ME

Hail Mary, full of grace,
The Lord is with thee.
Blessed art thou among women
And blessed is the fruit of thy womb, Jesus.

Holy Mary, Mother of God,
Pray for us sinners
Now and at the hour of our death. Amen

PROLOGUE

$\mathcal{I}$ am lying in bed shivering under the covers in a small Bosnian village where millions, maybe even billions, believe the Virgin Mary has been appearing for the past sixteen years. The recurring apparitions have become a magnet for believers from around the world. I, too, am here to see. I am on a silent fasting retreat with forty-nine zealous Catholics and haven't spoken or eaten anything besides bread and tea for days with the hope that if we are hungry enough, we will fill with God. And now, I guess because those deprivations are not enough, the wind just blew out the lights, and I'm stunned by the appropriateness of the symbolism: I may be on a religious retreat, but I am left in the dark.

I've come as a writer and have been going to chapel and lectures and church every day as part of the job, but I've also been praying to Mary, hundreds of Hail Marys, which is not part of the job. Then, to see how confession would feel, I made an appointment with the priest and have been lying in bed dreading what I will say. "Forgive me, Father, for I have sinned; it has been thirty-five years since my last confession.

I have slept with more men than I care to remember; I'm a selfish daughter and lousy mother whose grown son was damaged by neglect; and my default reaction to disappointment is despair." It seems impossible to actually say this.

I slink farther down under the covers and hear the line of a hymn, "Do not be afraid, I am with you," and break into tears. I weep when the wind screeching at the window wakes me in the middle of the night; I weep in the morning as I sit up in bed and stare at the rain dribbling down the glass; and I cry again in the little chapel where we meet for mass at noon every day when the lady with the doily on her head says, "For the poor and the lonely and the lost, let us pray." As the tears fall, I know I did not come here only to write about the experience; I came because I want Mary to mother me and teach me mother things, like how to love.

That evening I traipse through the gusting winds, praying on my rosary beads, then kneel in the village church with all the pilgrims. I wish and I hope and I pray for a little mustard seed of faith to move the mountain that is me out of the dark and into the light.

If you told me a year ago that this person looking for Mary and paraphrasing Christ was me, I would have fallen off my chair laughing.

CHAPTER ONE

S ix years before I landed in Bosnia, the Virgin Mary was no more than a dim memory, another fairy tale from my childhood as I sat in my rocker day after day, heartbroken over a man, but really over my life, which I thought of as pathetically impoverished. I was forty and alone and had just moved to a tiny village by the sea called Orient, where I knew nobody. I rocked and stared at the bay, which changed from midnight blue to battleship gray; then when I turned on the light I was horrified, and mesmerized, by my own reflection: my gray roots were an inch long (vanity hadn't fled with the onslaught of depression, just the energy to keep up any semblance of a beauty regimen); the creases that ran from the sides of my nose to the sides of my mouth made me look like a puppet; my eyes were hollow and sad. The man I was mourning, Kip, had insisted he still loved me, but he was a coward and he was lying. It wasn't only the physical that had repulsed him. It was the cold hard heart in the middle of me: too defended, too brittle, too pockmarked by life.

There'd been no soft pillow of comfort for him to sink into. No motherliness in me.

In the end, I'd been the one to leave, the way I'd left so many men, pridefully. Yet when I dropped Kip at Bradley International Airport, there'd been no pride left. I'd sobbed and gasped for breath. Kip's face was shiny with tears, too; both of us crying for the sweet promise we had and the sweet promise we had broken. He walked around to my side of the car and kissed me through the window; our faces were slippery with tears. Then, as he slung his backpack onto his shoulder, I took one last look at the familiar tilt of his neck, the loveliness of his body as he walked away, and my heart cracked, not like an egg but like a dried-up riverbed.

And so I rocked and I hugged myself as though the hypnotic rhythm, the pressure on my chest, would soothe away the hole of longing, coddle the ache in my heart, make me feel like a baby in the cradle of her mother's arms. Then I shut off the light and drifted to bed without brushing my teeth, or washing my face, or looking in a mirror, or doing anything with my hands besides squeeze them between my knees.

I'd been depressed before and was afraid if I didn't end it some way, this dark night of the soul could stretch on for years. A walk off a dock with rocks in my pockets seemed a good idea; but instead, for the New Year, I plunged into therapy—again.

"You have to learn to love yourself," said my new therapist, Eileen.

I needed to pay money to hear this? "And how do I do that?"

"Sometimes people find another person who loves them unconditionally, and then, because they feel loved, they can love themselves."

I'd say I'd been looking for that about half of the days of my life—okay, maybe a third; writing took up a lot of my time. I figured Kip was as close as I was going to get, and he'd kicked me in the heart. "Don't you have to love yourself before anyone's going to love you?" I asked rhetorically.

Eileen sidestepped the question. "Sometimes people find love through God."

"God?" Great—I'd signed on with an evangelist. "I hate God!" I almost yelled. "I grew up Catholic. Every time I stubbed my toe I had to figure out what I'd done wrong to deserve it. I spent five years in my first therapy trying to get rid of the guilt the Church put there. Oh, really." I shuddered. "I would just love to try to be perfect and beat myself up every night before bed, not only for the things I did but for the things I didn't do—and what I thought in my head. No thank you."

"A holy person," she redefined. "Spirit, Buddha, whatever you want to call it. And you reach them through meditating. Meditation works."

I'd always meant to meditate. I'd done affirmations till I was blue in the face, and I did believe that if somehow you could be given the unconditional love you didn't get when you really needed it, as a child, then you could heal. For me a holy person might be the only way, a last-ditch effort.

And so I began to meditate. I started with five minutes and did guided meditations, encouraged by Eileen, who'd suggested I try to imagine a spirit or a holy person. Mary? I thought about her. But she was too removed and sterile, too far away up in the virginal Catholic clouds. I couldn't sense her, or touch her. An embroidered Virgin of Guadalupe throw had, however, made it back with me from Mexico, where I'd lived with Kip. It was colorful with accents of gold and covered my computer like a good-luck charm. For a time, I pictured a young Persian-looking woman on a flying carpet who flew me around and bathed me in rivers. Eventually I settled on a little Buddha. I am a stone-cold statue abandoned in the woods and tangled in vines, and this little Buddha finds me there, loads me onto his cart, and wheels me into the sunshine in the middle of a beautiful garden. Then he begins chipping away the stone. First I feel the heat of the sun on my skin, then the breeze, which is fragrant with flowers. Very slowly I open my eyes, and the first thing I see is an emerald-green garden and, at its edge, purple flowers shaped like little trumpets, cascading to the ground.

By the spring, I'd been doing this meditation for a few months and felt adventurous enough one Saturday morning to drag myself out of bed at seven, wash my face, drink a cup of coffee, then head out for yard sales with the local paper in hand. I had only the set of table and chairs I'd dragged around with me since my teenage marriage home, the rocker I'd been glued to, a desk, a bed, a bureau, and a small advance to write a novel I hadn't even begun. So, I was really going on a furniture-scavenging excursion. My first stop was a contents-of-house sale, which usually means the owner has died. The place was a homely little aluminum-sided, post–Korean War affair, which I almost drove right by; but I made the decision to be open and not pass judgments. It was only seven-thirty and the sign said No Early Birds, but the husky little boy guarding the back door let me in. There were a few others already milling around the kitchen, whose cupboard contents had been piled onto the Formica table. I picked up a few shot glasses, because I had none, then walked into the living room.

The furniture was fake colonial and identical to my parents'. I pressed my hand to my chest to protect my heart. Would my siblings and I sell my mother's department-store dishes, my father's woodworking tools, virtually none of which we'd want for ourselves? Would we stand guard as people snatched the crocheted afghan from their couch, then watch it disappear out the door?

My parents were almost seventy; both of them smoked; and they were not in good health. Yet, with his chronically aching back, that fall my father had driven all the way from Connecticut to Vermont in his pickup truck to help me move. In New London we'd taken the ferry across Long Island Sound and had eaten grilled-cheese sandwiches, then strolled outside on the deck. My father's thick silver hair rippled in the breeze as he jangled the change in his pocket and we leaned on the rail, gazing out over the sound. "I always liked the water," he said.

"Me, too. I always wanted to live by the sea one day, and now I will."

"Atta girl."

When my father and I pulled up to my spindly old rented Victorian in Orient, a village on the northeasternmost tip of Long Island, my son, Jason who'd come from New York City to help us, was sitting on the step waiting. Jason had graduated college and was living in our old apartment on Avenue A. He was always on time and absolutely dependable, a good boy who'd never given me a moment's trouble. His hair, platinum and straight when he was a child, had been brown and wavy since high school. He was now twenty-three years old, over six feet tall, and, as a few of my younger women friends had let me know, a babe. My father and he patted each other's shoulders as they shook hands; then Jason kissed me on the cheek, "Hey, Mama."

I cupped my hand to his face, then kissed him too. "Hey, Jase."

We unloaded my few pieces of furniture, my boxes of dishes and linens, and my thirty-two boxes of books. I made us ham-and-cheese sandwiches with mustard, which we ate at the table in my new kitchen, followed by slices of the apple-walnut cake my mother had sent. I looked at them gratefully, the two men in my life. There were no others. My father had brought his toolbox, just in case, and it was a good thing. The wood around the hinges on my cellar hatchway had rotted, so my father moved them a few inches farther apart. He removed a door I didn't want between the kitchen and the dining room, and then at dusk I kissed them both goodbye in my driveway. "You take care now," my father said.

"Bye, Ma," my son said, looking worried.

This was the first time in my life I'd lived without my son or a man. The next morning, I'd headed for the rocker.

At the yard sale, I did not want to imagine how desperately alone I'd feel when my parents passed away, and nearly ran from that colonial furniture and up the stairs to the second floor, where, in a small bedroom on a nightstand next to a single bed, the Virgin Mary took my breath away. She was in a framed postcard as Our Lady of Fatima, dressed in a white luminescent gown, floating peacefully in a powdery gray, star-twinkled sky. Glitter graced her veil, and a single white rose sat on each foot as three little kids in babushkas knelt on a grassy hill, looking adoringly up at her, and I was struck by a powerful urge—the same feeling I get when I'm handed a furry kitten or an adorable baby: I just wanted to eat her up. Another shopper walked in and I grabbed that picture so fast you'd have thought I was a starving street dog who'd just been thrown a T-bone steak.

I hung that little picture in my bedroom next to the light switch; and the next Mary—a crosscut of a tree on which Mary in a varnished print looks concerned for *you* as she points to her own stabbed heart—I hung next to the mirror in the bathroom. A Rubenesque Mary looking knowingly at a chubby baby Jesus on her lap found a place above my bed.

I did feel love for Mary every time I looked at the paintings I'd begun to collect, but I was in love with my other yard-sale paintings, too. I had no idea that before long the Blessed Mother would multiply all over my house like

Richard Dreyfuss's little mud mountains in *Close Encounters of the Third Kind.*

But I get ahead of myself. As that little Mary postcard entered my house that first spring in Orient, Mary planted one little hook in my heart that let in one little ray of light, and Nancy Sawastynowicz, my new best friend, came in.

I'd seen a big blond woman with braids, digging across the road that spring; then, a few days after I found my first Mary, on my way home from buying coffee around the corner at the general store, the woman stabbed her spade in the earth, stood, and offered her hand. "I'm Nancy Sawastyn- owicz McCarthy," she said. "That's my son, Seth." She indicated a little boy on a tricycle down the road. "I had him late in life. I'm forty-one. I'm never having another." Her eyes sparked and I thought she might be looking for a joke, but I was still depressed and not in the mood.

I did, however, notice the coincidence. Nancy and I had both said, "I'm never having another," even though we'd had kids at the opposite ends of our lives. But I was still feeling separate and looking for differences, not similarities. I smiled and excused myself.

But blessings can be as persistent as curses, and Nancy refused to be discouraged. She knocked at my door later in the day, carrying a shovel and a shoebox. "I brought you some flowers from my mother's yard. You could plant them out back."

"They'll probably die."

"Nah. All they need's water and food."

She carried them through my kitchen and out the back door, so I followed her. "You got a spade?"

I shook my head.

"That's okay." She stabbed her shovel into the ground near the back fence. "I got an extra. You could have it."

"I couldn't."

"Why not?" She pulled two baby plants, joined at their roots, apart. "These are sweet williams. They'll do good here. Look, you got evening primrose coming up." She brushed some leaves away and I could see pale green shoots poking through the earth. I ran my hand over the little nubs. Had they been growing all through the winter in the dark and the cold? Nancy brushed away more leaves and began yanking out clumps of dead stalks. I'd had unremarkable vegetable gardens a few times, but I'd never grown flowers and wasn't sure I wanted to start. But I knelt beside Nancy and yanked too. Then, as she patted the sweet williams in the ground and watered them in, she said, "Did you read all those books I saw you carrying when you moved in?"

"Hell, no."

"I should have helped you."

"Why?"

"'Cause you needed it? I'm a DP—dumb Polack. I stayed back in the third grade. I can't spell."

"Spelling's overrated." I remembered from our earlier conversation that Nancy was a year older than I. Because she'd stayed back we probably had graduated high school in the same year. "I graduated in '68, too."

"Queen of the Prom." She jabbed her thumb at her chest.
"The Girl Who Got Pregnant." I jabbed my thumb at mine.
She howled. "You want a margarita?"

Nancy stopped by every day just to check in. If my dishes
were dirty, she did them. She swept the floor; she watered
my plants. "Sit down," I'd say. "I don't want to," she'd say
back.

We made dump runs together, waded into the bay to
clam, and rowed a boat out to scallop. We pedaled on our
bikes by the light of the moon, through bulrushes rustling by
our ears, past newly plowed fields that smelled of damp earth,
by choppy inlets we could hear lapping in the distance. When
the moon was full, we pedaled harder, and Nancy repeated
every few minutes, "I'm mooning, man." Back home we were
too stirred up to sleep, so we sipped tea in my kitchen and told
stories. Nancy had played piano and guitar when she was
younger and told me how she used to perform at teen mass.
"It was All Saints' Day; I play 'When the Saints Come
Marching In,' and they kick me out. It was All Saints' Day!
The morons. I never went back, not even when my cousin
Sissy got married; I stood outside the door."

The sky that winter could be overcast for weeks, allowing
not even a glimpse of the moon; but Nancy and I could tell
when the moon was waxing or waning by the tone of our
moods. The sea, the moon, the earth are all feminine, and
perhaps because you couldn't walk from your house to your
car without smelling or feeling them, there was a tradition of
powerful women in Orient. When whale oil still lit the
lamps of the world, the men left for long, two-year stretches

to hunt the seas for whales. The women worked the land; they grew the food, raised the children, chopped the wood to heat their houses. I had heard rumors that there was a coven of witches in Orient, which I tended not to believe, especially once I heard the same rumor about Nancy and me. I knew for certain, though, that there was an enclave of lesbians. Half of the land was still farmed in Orient, and from the time the asparagus appeared early in the spring till the pumpkins and squash came late in the fall, stands dotted the roads "manned" by women. In this woman-dominated world, the very air I breathed made me feel planted, grounded, rooted, sane.

While my house continued to fill with Marys (on a felt banner as the Virgin of Guadalupe, she stood at the top of the stairs; in a small bedroom I planned to turn into my shrine room, she was a regal queen wearing a jeweled crown, with all of humanity nestled in her cape), I went outside my third spring in Orient and started to dig. I dug a garden along the back fence and a plot twenty feet by six in the lawn. I pulled onion grass for so many hours that when I closed my eyes at night I saw the white bulbs traveling through the earth like sperm. The sun warmed the back of my neck as my fingers reached into the damp earth like they were roots themselves. I stayed out in the rain. I kneeled in the mud; I didn't answer the phone. I had new deadlines: a bed to dig, seedlings to transplant, mulching, watering, feeding to do.

One day late that third spring, when the chestnut blossoms on the trees had already faded, I came in at sunset after a full day's gardening and stood at the bathroom sink to wash my hands. I glanced at my face in the mirror and noticed for the first time that it was next to Mary's face on the varnished print. It looked like we were standing next to each other. Mary wore a mysterious half-smile as her hand gently pointed to the red heart on her sky-blue dress; flames shot out the top (passion); a sword went right through it (pain); tears dripped down (sorrow); but beautiful pink roses made a ring around it, too (joy, celebration, beauty, grace, redemption).

That heart told a story like a novel. It was just like life: complicated, changing, never the same. And Mary was showing this to me. I started to weep and didn't know why. But I think it was from gratefulness. My heart wasn't feeling so cracked anymore. It was feeling like one of Mary's hearts: a sword had pierced it, but roses encircled it, too.

That summer I grew a dozen herbs; Borghese, San Remo, and cherry tomatoes so sweet they gave me a sugar rush. I grew beans and peppers, lettuces, squash, garlic. My sunflowers grew taller than my clothesline pole; my basil plants were as high as my hip. The hollyhocks towered over my shed. And the Canterbury bells grew into the purple trumpet flowers from my meditations three winters ago. The purple trumpets grew so abundantly and for so long I thought that surely my envisioning them day after day had nourished the real flowers as much as the vision had nourished me.

One day Nancy brought her friend Anthony, who'd gone into the seminary, to my backyard, and he declared it a miracle. Anthony said I'd summoned the divas. I thought divas were opera singers, but he told me these devas, with an *e* not an *i*, were the helpers of fairies, and when they sense love being poured into the earth, they come and pour whatever nutrients the plants need into the soil.

I had no idea I'd summoned the devas, and I had no idea I'd summoned Mary, either. I'd made a shrine of my house, and knowing a good opportunity when she sees one, the Blessed Mother came in.

❦

In the sixth month the angel Gabriel was sent from God to a city of Galilee named Nazareth, to a virgin betrothed to a man whose name was Joseph, of the house of David; and the virgin's name was Mary. And he came to her and said, "Greetings, favored one! The Lord is with you." But she was much perplexed by these words and pondered what sort of greeting this might be. Then the angel said to her, "Do not be afraid, Mary, for you have found favor with God. And now, you will conceive in your womb and bear a son, and you will call him Jesus. He will be great and will be called the Son of the Most High.". . . Mary said to the angel, "How can this be, since I am a virgin?" The angel said to her, "The Holy Spirit will come upon you, and the power of the Highest will overshadow you; therefore, the child to be born will be holy; he will be called the Son of God. And now your relative Elizabeth in her old age has also conceived a son; and this is the sixth month for her who was said to be barren. For nothing will be impossible with God." Then Mary said,

"Here I am, the servant of the Lord; let it be with me according to your word." Then the angel departed from her.

—The Gospel According to Luke

Mary did not just fall down on her knees and submit to whatever the angel from God proposed to her. She wondered what exactly this angel was saying, so the angel rushed to assure her that she would not be the only one giving birth under miraculous circumstances. The angel had visited Elizabeth too; Elizabeth had been barren but was now pregnant. The young cousin and the old cousin would have babies six months apart; their children would both be prophets. Elizabeth's was John the Baptist. When Mary hears that she is not alone, that her cousin will accompany her on this strange journey—and no doubt give her strength and support—she takes heart. She believes that this angel in front of her is no hallucination, and courageously finds the faith to accept her fate. And so Mary says graciously, "Let it be . . . ," then wastes no time in departing to visit Elizabeth.

CHAPTER TWO

*O*n a stopover at the Rome airport on my way to Medjugorje, I spot a man holding a Mother Missions sign at the exit and head over. Most of my fellow pilgrims have arrived on a different plane, but a few had been on my flight, and I pass two of them at the luggage carousel. They're old ladies with tightly permed gray hair, whom I'd noticed on the plane by the Mother Missions name tags pinned to their crocheted vests. In fact, had I not changed from a window to an aisle at check-in, they would have been my seatmates, and I would not have ended up trapped next to a six-foot-tall Sicilian ex–soccer player who wouldn't leave me alone. Was I married? Did I have a boyfriend? Was he meeting me in Italy? I'd been forced to lie to shut him up, which was no way to start a religious retreat. And it hadn't worked, anyway. He'd reached over and grabbed my tableware to rip the plastic open for me, and when the lights went out he leaned his shoulder and then his head into mine, and his fingers tickled my thigh. I swatted his hands away and hung halfway into the aisle.

Thinking about this in the airport, I promise myself that

for the duration of this pilgrimage I am going to stop exert-
ing my will and practice surrendering—even as I rub my
hands like Lady Macbeth doing Out Damned Spot, and will
myself to stop scratching them. My hands have become in-
fested with blisters the size of fleas and are itching me like
mad. In New York before I left, my hands had gotten so bad
I couldn't sleep, eat, or think, and when a few of the bumps
turned brown and flattened to the size of nickels, I went to
the emergency room. The doctor looked it up in a book and
showed me a black-and-white picture of hands identical to
mine. It was not poison ivy, as I'd hoped, but a recurring
nervous condition for which there was no cure.

There were good reasons for my nervous reaction. My
idea had been that if I acted as though I had faith, then faith
would follow, and so I'd signed up for the only pilgrimage I
could find to Bosnia at a time I could get away: ten days in
Medjugorje, six of them at a no-talking-allowed retreat, during which we would fast on bread and tea and submit ourselves to brainwashing by a Franciscan with three advanced
degrees. Afterwards, we would go on a weeklong miraculous-
sites-of-Italy tour.

I'm afraid both that nothing will happen and that I'll experience a spiritual conversion that will turn me into a holy
person I won't even recognize, or have the desire to speak to.
It actually occurs to me that my hands are peeling themselves raw so new lines of identity can etch into my palms.

I rub my hands discreetly on my luggage as I reach the
man with the Mother Missions sign, who is being yelled at

by a woman with a pink plastic barrette placed asymmetrically above each ear. "We have to wait *nine* hours?" She slams a book against her thigh. A Bible?

I let her know I empathize by smiling at her, but she doesn't smile back. She looks at me as she continues to yell at the man. "You *planned* it this way?" She shakes her head as she walks away. "I just wish I'd have known."

"Oh, you're the journalist," the man says when I introduce myself. "I'm Bruce." Bruce, along with his wife, Annalena, are the organizers of the pilgrimage. We'd talked a few times on the phone.

"I'm not a journalist, I'm a writer," I clarify. "Journalist" makes me nervous. It implies objectivity, which I do not like to claim in the best of circumstances, and certainly not while I'm in the market for a spiritual conversion.

Bruce puts his hand on my arm. "Nobody goes to Medjugorje and comes back the same. You are in for the time of your life. Last year I climbed Mount Krizevac barefoot."

"Why'd you do that?" I have a hand-rubbing frenzy.

He blinks, confused by my inability to understand something that to him is so obvious, but he recovers. "Out of love for Our Lady. You'll see. You have no idea what you are about to experience."

A crowd has gathered, who all seem to wear glasses as big as windows and look like they feed from the snack aisle at the supermarket; half of them are in jogging suits. I close my eyes and pray: If only there were one other woman with lipstick. . . . I open my eyes and, I swear to God, there are two women with lipstick, wheeling a wide load of expensive luggage in my direction.

"Sisters?" I ask. They have something of a Mutt-and-Jeff thing going but are dressed almost identically in flower-patterned long skirts and silk knit sweaters, with tasteful pumps and manicures.

"Uh, huh. I'm Arlene," the short one says, "and this is Alma."

"Little Majesty"— Alma smiles, indicating Arlene—"and Little Sista—" she bows, indicating herself. The sisters have southern accents.

"You're the boss because you're older or shorter?" I ask Arlene.

"She's older and shorter, but that's not why she's the boss," Alma says. "Let's just say she's queenly. You'll see. And you?"

"I'm Beverly. Just call me the Lapsed Catholic. I'm a writer."

"How lovely," says Little Majesty.

The three of us become so involved talking, we spend the nine hours before we leave for Bosnia eating dry lasagna and sipping Cokes at the snack bar instead of taking a look around Rome. The sisters are mothers of grown children, too. The sisters had been raised Catholic by their Cajun grandma and single mother. While Little Majesty always stayed near home, Little Sista went far away to college. Both had been schoolteachers, but Alma was now the deputy superintendent of schools in her city, and Arlene had retired at fifty to do charity work sponsored by her wealthy businessman husband. Alma had divorced and remarried, yet received the holy sacrament of communion right next to her Presbyterian husband every Sunday—a sin, as defined by the Church and the intransigent Pope—and Arlene disapproves. "We're supposed to be obedient," Little Majesty intones, more wistfully than chidingly.

"Father Diego"—obviously Alma's pastor—"doesn't object. He knows I'm divorced. He knows John's not Catholic."

"We're not supposed to criticize our priests."

"Father Diego is a wonderful priest."

"I'm not saying he isn't. We'll just pray to Our Lady."

"Yes, Little Majesty."

"How old's your son, Beverly?" Little Majesty changes the subject.

"Twenty-eight."

"You must have been awfully young," says Little Majesty.

"I was."

"Like Our Lady," says Alma.

I lived in Orient for six years, and one night my last year there, I invited a new neighbor named Daniel to a dinner party, and after a tour of my house, I overheard him say to another man, "So what do you think of Beverly's Mary cathexis?" Daniel was a psychiatrist; his comment gave me a little jolt. So when he left, I looked "cathexis" up in the dictionary. It means: "Investment of mental or emotional energy in a person, object, or idea." Mary was all over my house; I had to admit I had a Mary cathexis. And a while later, when I finally asked Daniel his psychoanalytic opinion of my condition, he went further. "I think there's a restorative fantasy, an identification. Whereas Mary conceived in holiness and grace, you conceived in dishonor and disgrace"—which I had to admit was also true.

There had been no angel bearing greetings from God at my "annunciation," and never in a million years could I—at seventeen—have imitated what I thought of as Mary's gracious and wimpy bow-down response, "I am the handmaiden of the Lord." I didn't think I believed in God anymore; yet in my heart I was still a Catholic girl convinced that God had willed my pregnancy to ruin my life, that premature motherhood was my punishment for daring to have sex. I felt wounded and betrayed, and I was furious at him. Instead of Mary's famous "Let it be," I'd stomped and punched my stomach, I'd bumped my ass down stairs, yelling inside, "God, I hate you." Then I banned him from my life.

In 1968 abortion still was illegal, and in my small-town, working-class Connecticut world, I knew only one girl on the pill, and she'd been given it for menstrual cramps. When I got pregnant, they still injected your urine into a rabbit, and if the bunny died, you were doomed. I'd lied to my parents about where I was going and brought my urine sample to the lab, then went to my best friend's house to await the results.

Fay and I lay on her bed and stared at the ceiling. "You're really going to marry Ray?" she asked rhetorically. I was a senior in high school.

"What else am I going to do?"

I'd already told Fay how Ray had responded when I told him I thought I was pregnant on the swings at the drive-in. He'd said, "I love you so much," then got off his swing, pulled me to him, and sobbed into my neck. I was all Ray had. He lived alone with his mother, who'd let him know that the only reason he existed was because his father had come home after being drunk on the Bowery for two years and raped her. My heart ached when he'd told me that story. Ray was like a broken bird I'd found on a sidewalk. I wanted to mend his wing, drop bits of food into his mouth, nestle his wounded body in the crook of my neck. Poor sad Ray, a high-school dropout, the butt of jokes by his friends, a boy everyone called Bud. But, convinced by the greatest cliché in the book, I believed my love could transform him back into a Ray: he'd earn his high-school equivalency, become an apprentice at something, join a trade union, build things.

"Your parents aren't going to let you marry him." Fay turned her face from the ceiling to look at me.

My father was an Italian cop and the only son in a family of wild sisters. I was his first daughter, and he was determined to control me, the way he could not control his sisters. But by the time I'd reached puberty, I'd become the type of kid who, when given a Kennedy half-dollar as a present and told not to spend it—ever—marched straight into town the next day and bought a pair of movie-star sunglasses.

I don't know why I was like that, but the more my father tried to discipline me into being a good, obedient girl, the more I was determined to do whatever I damn well pleased.

And now—because I did not want to give my baby up for adoption and go through life forever imagining my lost kid—I was getting married.

"I'll elope," I told Fay defiantly.

But I kept wondering, Why me? It was so unfair. Maybe I never did homework, skipped school chronically, and had a wiseguy attitude; but I had potential. I was on the Student Council and in the Girls League. I was in a singing group. I gave speeches at assemblies. I starred in plays. But no boys ever asked me out, and no boys asked Fay out, either. We knew it was because we had big mouths and called things the way we saw them, which scared guys away. But deep in my heart, what I really believed was that I was unlovable and that I was lucky that even Ray—who was not cute or smart, clever, athletic, or strong—loved me.

Still, by the time I was a senior, one year after Ray and I had first gone out, I'd matured enough to recognize my own impatience. When I graduated high school I was moving to New York City to be an actress. In New York there'd be interesting and intelligent young men—artists and intellectuals—who might appreciate me. When I became rich and famous, they'd arrive in limos, bearing armfuls of roses, falling over one another to light my cigarettes. Eventually I'd marry one.

I'd been relieved when Ray started talking about joining

the navy. I was counting on sending him a Dear John in boot camp and taking my life back. But then I got pregnant.

I sat at the edge of the bed as Fay called for my results. She hung up the phone, knelt in front of me, and bowed her forehead to my knees. "Poor Bev," she said. "You're fucked."

I could not face my parents with the news, so I left a note in the mailbox on my way to school, and when I got home my father was crying at the kitchen table, while my mother leaned against the stove. She crossed her arms against her chest. "You proud of yourself now?" she said. "You put every gray hair on your poor father's head. You think you're going to be happy? You think having a baby's fun? You think it's easy? You think you're going to like putting somebody else before yourself?"

No. No. No. No. No.

Seven months later, I gave birth to my child, and there were no angels blowing trumpets, no magi visiting, no star to guide them in the sky. When I awoke from the anesthesia, the nurse held out my son swaddled in a blanket and said, "Congratulations, Mrs. Budrow, you have a healthy eight-and-a-half-pound baby boy."

"Boy!" I screamed. I'd been convinced I was carrying a girl and that she looked just like me. I think I'd wanted to give birth to myself. I looked at my baby's face. He was sucking his bottom lip, and his eyes were closed, but he was awake. This little person had been growing inside of me, feeding, kicking, rolling, giving me heartburn. I hadn't known it was he. He was a stranger. A boy. What would I do with him?

Ray wanted to name his son after himself, but I insisted on Jason after a character on a TV show. "Jason" does sound a little like "Jesus," but I can promise you I didn't make the connection.

Five days after Jason's birth, Ray and I brought our baby home to our little duplex on a dead-end street across from a fireworks factory. My mother was there with the marble cake she'd baked; my father and sisters were waiting too. The place almost glittered from the cleaning my mother had given it; the bottles she'd sterilized were drying upside down on top of paper towels. Everyone took a turn with Jason; but when they left, and Ray fell asleep, I was alone with my baby son. The vulnerable, soft circle at the top of his head; those tiny toes with nails no bigger than a match head; his bouncy penis that would go erect; the wrinkly walnut sacs of his testicles; the smell of him: I was overwhelmed by his presence and terrified by his need for me.

But like a new puppy, Jason grew on me within a day, and I fell in love. I rocked him alone in the house, intoxicated by his baby smell, the squirmy warmth of his little body, his skin as soft as a bubble. I could not stop kissing him. I was fascinated by his tiny hand gripping my finger as he drank his bottle. My eyes followed his hand as it let go, then drifted weirdly through the air with no destination or reason—or was it looking for something more solid to hold on to?

After I burped him, his faint breath next to my ear as we

rocked made me sleepy, and I lay on the floor with his body like an eternal hug on my chest.

We were napping like this one afternoon when the doorbell rang, and I answered it to a salesman selling a set of knives that came with a clock that had scenes from the life of Jesus and Mary in six circular pictures around the walnut frame. I bought the knives but hated the ugly proselytizing clock. And I hated Mary. I despised her abdicating her will to God's. Not that I'd believed in her since puberty, but she was a figurehead for a mythology I wanted nothing to do with: woman as ever-loving wimp.

I threw the clock in the garbage, then pulled a sack of potatoes from under the sink, filled a pot with water, and brought it all, along with my new paring knife, into the living room. I strapped Jason into his little tilted chair, which I bounced with my foot as I peeled potatoes on an aluminum snack tray, dropping the peels onto soggy newspaper while watching *Days of Our Lives.*

When I finished with my peeling, I dumped the potato peels on top of the Holy Mother and Son, then slammed the lid down.

I may have wanted nothing to do with the Holy Mother but was very lucky to have my own flesh-and-blood mother nearby. My parents lived a mile away, and Jason and Ray and I ate dinner at their house at least three times a week. We watched television with my sisters, and my mother often washed our clothes. But by the time Jason was six months old, Ray and I had discovered marijuana and made a break for independence. It was now 1969; I listened to albums all day long, smoked endless cigarettes, buried myself in books my girlfriend loaned me from her college classes. While I threw away my bras and started to write poems, Ray grew his beard and longed for a motorcycle. After we were married a year, and Jason was seven months old, Stephen was laid off from the fiberglass factory, and we considered it a stroke of good fortune. He'd receive unemployment. We could hang together, drive to Hubbard Park to feed the ducks with Jason, take turns going out with our friends while the other baby-sat.

But then one night, Ray said he was going to his friend Jimmy's house and came home the next day with a tattoo of a devil holding a pitchfork illuminating his forearm. That was only the first little betrayal. There were many more, more than there were records in our collection or ten-dollar bills stashed in our attic for a rainy day. When I wasn't paying attention, Ray had become a junkie; he'd broken into houses and stolen things. He and his friends had taken turns tying off and shooting up in our bathroom, while I'd baked jelly muffins in the kitchen—which they never ate because they were too high. Ray spent every dime of our savings; he robbed Jason's piggy bank.

When I threw Ray out, Jason was thirteen months old and napping in his room. Ray stuffed his clothes into two pillowcases; then turned to me with his hand on the doorknob. "I love you, Beverly. I always have."

There were tears in Ray's eyes. When I said nothing, he continued. "I'm no good. You shouldn't have loved me."

I'd nursed him through one withdrawal and I'd told him

if he ever used heroin or lied again, our marriage would be over. When I caught him walking out the door with Jason's savings bond—a gift from his baptism—sticking out of his back pocket, it was all finished for me. Still, I felt my heart collapsing under a waterfall of memories: Ray's large hands tenderly soaping Jason's tiny back as he bathed him in the kitchen sink . . . Ray with his ears sticking out from a new haircut, looking so scared and young at the bottom of the aisle, waiting for me at our wedding . . . his eyes playful with desire in our living room, crowded with our friends. (I allow my knees to fall open to give him a peek; then later, in the kitchen, he pushes me against the counter, his hands like little tickly animals under my skirt.) . . . Ray slapping his hands to his eyes when I tell him our best friend, Dickie, has died in Vietnam—how I rocked my husband, and how we cried together as he moaned, "My buddy, my buddy . . ."

Remembering, my tears filled my eyes, and I wished I'd loved him more, better, truly—then, the next second, my heart wrung into a fist of self-protection, and I was responding to his woe-is-me "You shouldn't love me" with "No shit."

I locked the door behind him.

A few months later, Ray volunteered for Vietnam, where heroin was abundant and cheap, and although I eventually heard he'd returned from the war, he never returned to live in our town, never supported us, and never was a father to his son.

Jason was too young when his father left to remember him. But as he grew older, in a way Jason took over the role of father in our little family of two. Jason tried to get me to follow rules, to put on my blinker at corners, to stay stopped at traffic lights when there was no other car in sight, to pay bills on time, to stop smoking marijuana. His constant refrain was "Why can't you be normal?" But I was stuck in a state of arrested adolescence, and because I no longer had a father or a husband in the house to rebel against, I rebelled against Jason.

But we had fun too. We sang and we danced. I let my little Volkswagen fly over bumps to give him and his friends a good ride. We visited cows and sat still by a green pond waiting to see the frogs' eyes pop through the surface.

The frog pond was on the ride to Wesleyan University, where I'd won a scholarship when Jason was six and I was twenty-four. We moved to campus, and while my neighbors and I organized cooperative meals, day care, and carpools, Jason and his new friends became vegetarians together, put on plays, roamed the campus like it was their own backyard.

My best friend, Susan, and Jason's best friend, Kitty, Susan's daughter, lived a few doors down. We ate together almost every night. We went to Crystal Lake in the summers, drove down to the beach, ate picnics on the table in Susan's backyard. When Susan graduated, a year ahead of me, and she and Kitty moved to New Haven, Jason and I were bereft. We sat on our porch and drank Cokes.

"You sad, Jase?" I asked him.

"Yeah. We'll visit them, though. Right?"

"Of course. What do you think you liked most about Kitty?"

"She's smart. We could talk. What did you like about Susan?"

"She's smart. We could talk. And dance."

"Kitty and I used to get mad."

"Why?"

"That Stevie Wonder song, over and over. Mom, you knew it made us mad."

"We didn't play it because it made you mad. We played it because we loved it."

"A thousand times?"

"You liked it, too—admit it." Jason and I had danced since he could stand on two feet, and we'd danced to *Songs in the Key of Life* almost every night for an entire winter.

"Kitty thought like me. We liked the same things. Little Ron drove us crazy."

"You're both pretty serious for kids. Why do you think?"

"I've always been serious."

"You think it's because I'm not?"

"Maybe. But you're more serious than Melanie." Melanie was Little Ron's mother, who never went to class, drank in the mornings, and wandered around campus barefoot.

Susan, a gifted painter, had found a job in New Haven selling ad time at a radio station. I was entering my senior year and didn't know what I'd do when I graduated, but could not imagine giving up my writing as she'd given up her painting. I wanted to move to New York City and be a poet or a novelist, but I had just enough money to put gas in my car every week, and had no idea how I'd ever save enough to move.

At the end of that summer before my senior year, a new family rented Susan and Kitty's house next door. They had a coal-black, adorably affectionate little puppy with floppy ears, named Max, with whom Jason and I fell instantly in love. We'd hear Max whining in the night from our windows and would cover our heads with our pillows. Then one night Jase came into my room. "Mom," he said, "I can't stand it. Poor Max. He's afraid of the dark. Can't we bring him in? Once? Please?"

And so we did, more than once. In the dark, we sneaked into our neighbor's backyard and brought Max up to Jason's room, then brought him back down at dawn.

Then, one day late in September, I came home from classes, and Jason ran into the house behind me. "Mom! Max is dead. He got hit by a truck."

"Oh, no." I sat on the couch. Jason sat beside me. We looked at each other and burst into tears. As we hugged and patted each other's backs, my friend Cindy showed up. When we told her what had happened, she said, "Let's do the Ouija." I'd bought Jason a Ouija board for his ninth birthday the week before, but Jase was already tired of it. So he went back out to play, while Cindy and I balanced the board on our knees, then lightly rested our fingers on the magic indicator and asked, "Max, are you there? Max, are you there?"

The magic indicator zipped from G to 6—G 6; G 6—with such force we jerked our hands to our faces. "Oh, my God!" Cindy blurted. "OTB, sixth race, G horse." Cindy had just come from the newly opened OTB. I'd never heard of the place before and had never bet on a horse in my life.

Yet the next day Cindy, Jase, and I placed all our money (Cindy twenty dollars, Jason two dollars, and I, forty dollars) on Siwache Chief—the long shot at eleven to one. The three of us listened to the radio in Cindy's kitchen; when it got down to the wire, we held hands—then jumped up and down screaming when Siwache Chief won. Jason was already good at math and kept saying, "Twenty-two dollars . . . twenty-two dollars!" Then, "Oh, my God, Mom—*you* won four hundred and forty-four dollars. That's more money than we ever had in our lives."

Of course, Cindy and I went right back to the board the next day, and this time we were given three more letter-number combinations. When each one of them scratched—which means the horses didn't even run, so we got our money back—we took it as a sign that we'd been given our one big win as a gift and should not be greedy for more.

The $444 was the nest egg I used to finance our move to New York the next fall. I thought of the move as a gift ordained by supernatural forces. I have sometimes thought that "G-6" sounds a lot like "Jesus," but I have also learned that six is the devil's number, and have come to believe that New York was our descent into hell.

❦

In those days Mary set out and went with haste to a Judean town in the hill country, where she entered the house of Zechariah and greeted Elizabeth. When Elizabeth heard Mary's greeting, the child leaped in her womb. And Elizabeth was

*filled with the Holy Spirit and exclaimed with a loud cry,
"Blessed are you among women, and blessed is the fruit of your
womb. And why has this happened to me, that the mother of my
Lord comes to me? For as soon as I heard the sound of your greeting, the child in my womb leaped for joy. And blessed is she who
believed that there would be a fulfillment of what was spoken to
her by the Lord."*

> *And Mary said,
> "My soul magnifies the Lord,
> and my spirit rejoices in God my Savior,
> for he has looked with favor on the
> lowliness of his servant.
> Surely, from now on all generations will call me blessed;
> for the Mighty One has done great things for me,
> and holy is his name.
> His mercy is for those who fear him
> from generation to generation.
> He has shown strength with his arm;
> he has scattered the proud in the
> thoughts of their hearts.
> He has brought down the powerful from their thrones,
> and lifted up the lowly;
> he has filled the hungry with good things,
> and sent the rich away empty. . . ."*

—The Gospel According to Luke

*The Magnificat is Mary's longest speech in the Bible, and it
is pure Mary. Her words are a paean to the unexpected, the*

world turned upside down, a hymn of encouragement to the disenfranchised, a reason to take heart. Mary was a Jew in Roman-occupied lands; she would marry a man who could not own land, which placed them at the very bottom of the social heap. But Mary knew that the poor and the lowly were blessed to the Lord.

This was a belief her son would share. Jesus would be schooled in Judaism, but he would also receive an earful from his mother. Jesus had a mission and Mary wanted to steer him straight.

CHAPTER THREE

*W*hen we debark our plane in Bosnia, the night is eerily dark, and spitting spurts of chilly wind. I feel a little foolish as I pull on my shiny black, three-quarter-length patent-leather jacket made in Italy and bought in New York City, instead of the waterproof parka we'd been advised to bring. And as I pass my reflection in a window heading for the bus, I'm afraid I resemble an SS officer. Namik, a Bosnian war refugee I'd become friends with when I moved to Los Angeles a year ago, had told me that the area of the country Medjugorje occupied spawned the worst Nazi war criminals. Could that be why Mary chose this place—did she know when she began to appear that six years later a bloody civil war would break out?

I'd lost the sisters in the scurry to stash our luggage and board the bus. As I mount the bus steps alone, I wonder whether I should take notes. But then I think, my fellow pilgrims have come for a religious experience and don't need to feel spied on by a woman in a shiny black leather SS coat. I've come for a religious encounter, too, and documenting every moment would get in the way of experiencing it fully emotionally.

I spot our priest, Father Freed, sitting alone toward the front of the bus. I'd seen him before at the airport—a small man in a nylon ski jacket and priest's collar; a shock of white hair and a youthful face. He's at least a couple of inches shorter than I, and his feet are so tiny they might be smaller than my hands—one of which I offer to him, then pull away, remembering my rash. "My hands," I apologize as I sit next to him. "Don't worry, it's not contagious. It's from nerves," I blurt. "I'm not even Catholic. I'm not even sure I really believe."

Luckily, I'm interrupted by Annalena, who has stood next to the driver, brushing her platinum-blond bangs from her face. "Listen up. This is the last leg. I know it's been a long haul. Just two more hours and we'll be in Medjugorje. Offer it up." What does that mean? She sounds like a gym teacher.

"So, how is it you're going to Medjugorje?" Father Freed asks me.

As I run through my story, I begin to feel more comfortable, like I'm talking to a regular guy and even flirting a little. When I get to the part about all the Marys in my house, I tell him how I've read that the early Eastern Church had forbidden the use of images to inspire devotion, but couldn't control it and finally approved their use. The images inspired uneducated people who could not read. For me it had been the opposite. I'd been too educated, had an overly analytic mind, and needed an image to help me feel what I felt, to let myself know what I knew unintellectually—that there is something going on out there, something beyond my senses that I want to know and even long for. I tell Father Freed how when I took a trip to Ireland my last summer in Orient I'd rented my house to a couple with a two-year-old daughter. They'd tried to put her to sleep in my shrine room and the little girl had freaked out until her mother took all the Mary pictures down.

Father Freed laughs.

Which encourages me. I tell him how after I left Orient, a year ago, I'd made a radio documentary in which I'd gone to Mary apparition sites around the country. People had told me to pray the rosary, and I did, for the radio story, as I tell Father Freed, "to see what would happen. I think something did happen. I say Hail Marys all the time, and it's a comfort. But I'm still a skeptic. I guess that's why I'm here: to see if I can believe."

I don't tell Father Freed that I think belief can be like yoga. I'd started taking yoga classes when I'd moved to LA, and at the beginning of class the teacher would say, "Stand in Mountain and spread your toes." My toes wouldn't spread. I didn't even know what it would feel like to spread my toes. But I stood there, every class, looked at my toes, and said, "Spread." Then one day they did. I thought if I kept praying, belief in God might happen like that.

Father Freed, who's been leaning toward me, with his head bent, nodding, says, "You know, it's said that if you're looking for God you've already found him. Just try to be open. Keep an open heart and mind. You may be surprised what happens."

"I hated the way the Church made me feel about myself."

"A lot of people had that reaction."

"But you didn't?"

"I always loved church. I was the youngest of four boys. Always liked to help my mother, was the peacemaker. Never rebelled against going to mass, never rebelled against anything. I've always loved God and felt that he loved me."

"Did you always want to be a priest?"

"Oh, no. I didn't become a priest till I was forty-five."

"No kidding?"

"I was a high-school science teacher. Had my own house, built it myself. I loved to travel. Used to lead tours to Europe summers. Had girlfriends, but never longer than two years. I could never commit. I was one of those. I would always come to a point that as much as I liked the woman's company it wasn't fair to keep her. I was active in the church, and I was in my forties and never married, so our pastor suggested I might like to be a priest. I thought about it, but my mother was getting on in years and I wanted to be near her. Then she got MS and her physical requirements were too much for me to take care of, so she went into a home and I said to myself, I'm going to take a philosophy of religion course and if I do well in it, I'll become a priest. I got an A. I was seeing a woman at the time and had to tell her I was going into the seminary. It had to be better than telling her I was seeing another woman. But maybe I'm wrong.

"When I was ordained, my mother came from the nursing home in a wheelchair. The bishop said, 'Now go get a blessing from your mother.' It broke me up. She died last year."

I liked this guy. "I heard you were given the gift of heal-ing?"

"Yes. Father Jozo came to the States, and I went to a serv-ice." Jozo was one of the priests in Medjugorje sixteen years ago when the visions began. He now has a church several towns away. "Father Jozo laid on hands, and I was slain in the spirit."

"What?"

"You never heard of 'slain in the spirit'? The priest puts his palm on your forehead and prays, and you feel the Holy Spirit enter you. I felt a sensation that was almost electrical running through me and I fell to the floor. It was very pleas-ant. I'd never experienced anything like that before. I'd suf-fered from chronic pain in my lower back for years. That just disappeared. After that, I came to Medjugorje the first time and visited Father Jozo's church. He has all the priests join him at the altar for mass; then afterwards people come up, and you lay on hands. I found I have a gift, and not just for physical healing. There was a woman who came to church after being away for many years and asked to speak to me. She was a very unhappy, bitter person, so disappointed in her life, blaming everyone, full of hate. But she let God in and everything changed. . . . She even got married."

We both laugh.

"Are you going to lay on hands on this trip?"

"I don't know."

"You should." It crosses my mind to ask Father Freed to bless my hands right then, but I can't do it; I'm too embar-rassed. It actually flits across my mind that I could be receiving the stigmata, the wounds of Christ that manifest themselves in hysterics and saints. Then Bruce interrupts, calling out, "Father Freed, would you lead us in a rosary?"

Those who already don't have rosary beads twined in their fingers (maybe only me) take them out. Mine are the blue plastic beads that Mrs. Sabatini, a woman at one of the apparition sites I'd visited for the radio piece, had given me in Queens. I close my eyes and try to concentrate on every word, then fall asleep during the second decade. When I awake some time later, the bus is silent, and Father Freed is asleep, too. I'd been leaning toward his warmth and my knee is pressing into his. I move it away and remember the soccer player on the plane. Might he really have been sleeping and naturally, innocently, leaned in toward human warmth?

As we pass through Mostar, out the window I can see large barrooms filled with black-clad, good-looking young people with cool hair, sitting at round tables drinking beers and smoking. I'm in a bus filled with plain and overweight Americans with rosaries in their laps. I'd been praying to the Virgin Mary when I fell asleep, and before that I'd been talking to a priest. And at this moment, my rosary in my peeling palm, Father Freed asleep beside me, I suddenly think, I wouldn't change places with those gorgeous young people for anything in the world.

The bus groans to a stop on a narrow road next to a stone wall. There are no streetlights and no moonlight, but soon we see a flashlight bouncing down the lane. It's Josef, the owner of House 2, where I've been assigned to stay with a roommate named Beatrice Day. I have lost sight of the sisters and wish I could see the cows I smell nearby, but it's too dark. My fat green suitcase keeps falling on its side in the rock-studded dirt road, and the women dragging their luggage all around me make supportive asides, "Ooopsy Daisy, hope nothing broke."

Our host, Josef, is joined by his wife, Mariana, at the door to their house. They're a tall young couple, surprisingly cheerful considering we've arrived past midnight. Josef points us down halls, saying, "Come, eat when you are ready. Soup. Below." Josef and Mariana had added onto their house and turned it into a guest house, which they fill with crowds of pilgrims like us.

It was in 1981 that the Virgin Mary began appearing to six kids, four girls and two boys in Medjugorje, which is in the former Yugoslavia, a country where East meets West, on what is now called Apparition Hill. The local clergy disapproved, the Communists tried to squash the apparitions; but the kids persisted—and so, presumably, did Mary, who talked to them like clockwork every afternoon. As always happens where Mary visits, word spread like holy fire, and the masses came. They somehow busted through the Eastern Bloc, and millions dodged bullets to come see her. I have read that not one bomb fell on Medjugorje, not one villager was injured, and a fighter jet was spun out of the sky when it dared fly above the town.

By the time I arrived, in late October 1997, sixteen million had come before me. Countless people, including clergy, claimed physical, emotional, spiritual healings; but it seemed a miracle in itself that the place had remained a peasant village and was not filled with high-rise hotels. The villagers had simply made their homes bigger and welcomed pilgrims, at a reasonable price, as their guests.

There's a tradition of Mary's conveying "secrets" to seers, who are most often children. Children still believe in magic and readily believe they're seeing Our Lady. They are also more likely to repeat her messages without staining them with their own interpretations. Perhaps the most famous visitation was in Fatima, Portugal, of which Medjugorje has been accused of being a copycat apparition. Remember, it was a little picture of Our Lady of Fatima that had been my first yard-sale find. In my picture—and, of course, in Fatima—Mary appeared to three little peasant kids, carrying her own string of rosary beads draped over her arm, imploring them and the world to pray the rosary to bring peace. It was 1917, at the peak of the First World War and the beginning of the Russian Revolution. Mary conveyed three secrets to the kids. One foretold the end of the First World War; another predicted the spread of communism. The third remained secret until the year 2000, when the Vatican finally revealed that the secret was a vision of the 1981 assassination attempt on Pope John Paul II. In 1946, a tenth of the population of Portugal gathered in Fatima to thank Our Lady of Peace for the end of the Second World War.

There are ten secrets in Medjugorje that will be revealed at some future time. As soon as the visionaries, all of whom were now adults, received ten secrets, Mary stopped appearing to them every day and appeared only on their birthdays and on special occasions. When I visit Medjugorje, two still have daily visions of Mary, and another, Mirjana, has a vision each month. The bishop of the region is in denial, but the local priests have become enthusiastic believers.

In her monthly messages, which can be read on the website out of Medjugorje on the Internet, Mary has made it known that she considers all people of all religions her children. She asks them to pray, but she also asks them to fast, and to attend daily mass and monthly confession—a lot to expect of a non-Catholic, but perhaps, like a mother, she thinks there's no harm in asking. Annalena, our pilgrimage leader, had been a lapsed Catholic. She had been working as a detective and a horse trainer when she was stricken with multiple sclerosis, which rapidly deteriorated her nervous system, so that within a few years she was a paraplegic. One trip on a stretcher up Mount Krizevac—a local mountain at whose top a huge cement cross had been erected during a drought at the turn of the century to consecrate the village to Mary—and Annalena was on her feet, fully functioning, and utterly converted. She and her husband, Bruce, also a cop, left their lives as they knew them to dedicate their new lives to Mary.

I stash my suitcase in my room, which has two single beds, a closet, and a bathroom. There's no other luggage and no Beatrice Day. I wash my hands and go directly to the dining room, where three urns of soup and baskets of thickly sliced bread are waiting in the middle of a long table.

I'm the first to sit down, feeling famished. Besides Father Freed, there are three single men on the pilgrimage and a half-dozen husbands and wives. That leaves thirty-two women, sixteen of whom file in around the table, including, to my re-

lief, the southern sisters, Arlene and Alma. A group is forming to walk up Apparition Hill after dinner. Bruce will lead
the way and will come by in an hour or so to see if anyone
wants to join.

I'd been on a plane, stuck in an airport, or cramped on a
bus for the last sixteen hours. And even though I'll be walking around the countryside after one in the morning, I decide the fresh air and exercise will do me good. Besides, I'd
read that Apparition Hill offered a good view of the cross
atop Mount Krizevac, and I'm hoping to see it glow like so
many have before me.

After downing the chicken soup, I find my flashlight and
drop it into my pocket, then walk out into the dark and
wait. I'd already taken a dislike to one woman, Jane, who'd
been a travel agent and had given everything up to move to
Conyers, Georgia, to be near Nancy Fowler, an apparition-
ist, and to care for the site grounds. I'd been to Conyers for
the radio documentary and did not like Nancy Fowler's
doom-saying messages: do not watch TV, avoid homosexu-
als, end abortion, or armies of Chinese soldiers will tromp
all over American soil. Fowler, like all the apparitionists,
claimed to be channeling the words of the Virgin Mary, but
this was not the Mary I wanted to know. While my producer
and I were reporting in Conyers, we'd talked to a brain sur-
geon who'd done extensive tests on Fowler. He said that
Fowler, like most apparitionists, went into a trance, which
measured metabolically as a coma. But unlike a person in a
coma, the seer is fully conscious and functioning. He'd
placed Fowler on one side of a divided room and another ap-

paritionist on the other side. Without being able to see or hear each other, both registered a coma at exactly the same time they claimed that Mary was in the room.

At dinner I'd overheard Jane, the woman from Conyers, talking about a statue that was bleeding in upstate New York, of a painting that was crying in Chicago or somewhere, and how the United States government is secretly preparing for the Chinese invasion at a base in San Diego. I could not keep my mouth shut. I said, "I just don't think Mary means to spread fear and terror."

"She's not the one spreading fear and terror. It already exists. She's just warning us. Nancy Fowler—"

"I'm sure Nancy Fowler does get these messages. But people, these seers, are human. They're fallible." I wanted to say that for all we knew, some of them could be channeling the devil disguised as Mary, but was afraid my tongue would burst into flames.

"We should wait and ask Father Slavko what he thinks," suggested Little Majesty, Arlene, the peacemaker. Father Slavko, the Bosnian priest who would lecture us daily, has a Ph.D. in psychology, which would serve us well, I hoped.

Jane and I had glared at each other down the long table. Now, as I stand outside waiting in the dark, she comes out the door with her flashlight. "Where are you from?" she asks.

"Los Angeles." I hate saying that without qualification, like "but for only a year." But this time I let her draw whatever conclusions she wants.

Another woman, very pretty and very heavy, joins us. I'd

noticed her in the airport, helping an old woman with a metal cane. She has dark hair that seems to have been set with rollers, perfect skin, blue eyes. "I am so excited," she says. "This is my first time."

"My third," says Jane. "Our Lady really wanted me to come. I had no money, but I knew if I prayed and asked and she wanted me to come she'd arrange it. Mr. Kane—he was a Protestant like me—visited Conyers and never left. His wife divorced him last year. He really wanted to come to Medjugorje, and one day—I hadn't said a word to him—he comes up to me and says, 'Would you like to come to Medjugorje? I don't want to go alone. I'll pay your way.'"

"Our Lady is so generous. I manage a bank and I couldn't leave," the heavy woman tells us. "I'm Beatrice Day, by the way."

"You're my roommate," I say to her.

"Oh, how do you do?" She sounds polite but not enthusiastic. "My assistant manager had been transferred," she continues, "and I was training a new girl, but I prayed to Our Lady. I knew she wanted me to come. I bought the ticket, even though I couldn't leave, and a week before our departure date, the old assistant manager came back. Just till after the New Year."

"Our Lady is so wonderful." Jane smiles.

It's my turn, but I don't want to play; and Our Lady must have been watching out for me, because I am rescued by the appearance of three other women stepping out of the house, followed shortly by the hectic woman with the smudged glasses and messy hair who'd been yelling at Bruce at the airport. In a minute, Bruce and eight or so others, holding bobbing flashlights, walk down the lane toward us.

Bruce leads us through vineyards to the base of a hill that has a wide path cobbled with juttings of limestone. We climb about the length of a football field before we reach the top, where a tall, slender, homemade wooden cross stands to mark the spot where Mary first appeared to three of the six kids. We sit on the rocks and I close my eyes. The wind has begun to pick up and the air smells clean and good; people begin to pray. A lovely woman with fine features and a melodic voice begins, "Thank you, Mother, for the blessings you have generously bestowed on each one of us. We are so thankful for this opportunity to be near you, we hope that—"

"Oh, dear God, look—look over on Mount Krizevac!" Jane interrupts.

Over on the mountain, lights streak the air. "Heavenly Mother, thank you, thank you for this sign. We love and adore you. We are so grateful to be near you. Help us open our hearts to hear your wishes. We—"

Could those jagged links of light really be a sign?

Now everybody's jumping onto the end of everybody else's prayer, impatient to begin her own. Then they begin singing some song I don't know. I switch from one uncomfortable rock to another and note that there are three men among us, but it's the women leading the prayers—straight from the heart, the way the women have probably always led the prayers when it's religion at the grass roots, outside of the physical and doctrinal walls of the Church. I also notice that the heavy hectic woman from the airport stands apart, not singing, like me.

"Look," someone says. "There are more lights coming up the mountain." Then there's a flash, obviously from a camera. "It's flashlights and cameras," someone says. Then Jane begins to pray again: "Thank you, Blessed Mother, for allowing us to believe it was a miracle," and is followed by a chorus of "Amen"s.

I'd been to apparition sites around the United States for the radio documentary and I should have been used to this. Almost to a person, the people I'd interviewed had been given signs: they'd seen gold dust rain, rose petals fall, rosaries and medals turn gold, the sun spin and change colors, flocks of doves appear in the sky, smelled the air fill with the fragrance of roses.

I'd seen their golden rosary beads, their Polaroids of what appeared to be a door in front of the sun with rays shooting around it that they called the "Doorway to Heaven." And at my first apparition site, I'd seen doves fly. It was the previous February, near the Unisphere on the grounds of the 1965 World's Fair, in Queens. Two hundred people had gathered around a makeshift stage on which a five-foot-tall, pure white statue of the Virgin Mary stood, on a night dark as ink. Little bursts of icy wind made people's scarves flap as they hugged their coats to them and huddled around votive candles they'd lit and placed on the ground around pictures of loved ones at their knees.

I'd gazed up at the sky, searching for a sign of anything.

Planes crisscrossed low, landing or taking off at JFK and La Guardia as the Long Island Expressway roared a few hundred yards to the right.

After David Isay, my producer in the radio documentary, had set up his recording equipment, a little lady in a fat down coat, named Mrs. Sabatini, walked over to tell us her story. "I got a sick daughter I take care of. And one day I started to bleed. You know, down there. Bleeding and bleeding. So I go to the doctor. He says I'm hemorrhaging and I got to go to the hospital. 'I can't go to the hospital,' I says, 'I got to take care of my daughter.' If I don't go to the hospital, he says, I'm gonna die. I got to talk to the Blessed Mother, ask her what I should do. So I come here on a bus all the way from Hartford. I get off and crawl on my belly to the Blessed Mother, I'm so weak. I say, Mary, what should I do? And the bleeding stops. The doctor said he never seen anything like it. Says I should've been dead. And there ain't nothing wrong with me. I'm cured."

When David walked off with his microphone to record ambient sound, Mrs. Sabatini leaned toward me and asked, "Why are you here, honey?"

I answered as honestly as I could. "I don't know. I began to collect her—you know, at yard sales—and the next thing I knew she was all over my house . . . beautiful paintings and statues. I liked her when I was a kid. Then I got the idea for this story."

"She's calling you." Mrs. Sabatini squeezed my arm. "Pray the rosary. It'll change your life. Here." She took a string of blue plastic rosary beads out of her pocket and handed the rosary to me.

"I couldn't."

"Go on. We make them, my girlfriend and me."

"The graces," said Mr. Schiavone, a friend of Mrs. Sabatini's who'd been listening in.

"What do you mean exactly by 'graces'?" I asked him.

"Gifts. Like peace. I feel peace," said Mr. Schiavone. "I pray to her. I go to church every day. I'm not mad at anybody anymore. I don't hate."

"Hate feels awful, honey. And you're not afraid no more," said Mrs. Sabatini. "Our Lady is wonderful," she said as she led me to the scapulars and pulled one from a box. "Wear this every day. You want it on when you die; that way Our Lady will protect you. Nail a cross to your door facing out so the earthquakes won't touch your house."

I gratefully draped the scapular on my neck, and before I could say thank you there was an explosion of camera flashes as people pointed to the sky and called, "The doves—it's the doves! Thank you, thank you, Blessed Mother. Oh, they're beautiful. Look at them. Look!"

A flock of doves swooped above the statue of Our Lady, circled once, and flew off; then another flock, and another, did the same.

"They were pigeons," David said at a diner we stopped at before driving back to New York.

"Pigeons are part of the dove family. And besides, they don't fly at night." I surprised myself by how much I wanted to believe I'd seen a miracle.

Afterwards, at my friend Robin's, where I was staying while in the city, I told her what had happened and she screeched,

"My God, what if it's real? Oh, Beverly . . ." Robin suddenly looked wistful. "I could use a mother."

"The thing is," I said, "the people I talked to had maxed out on pain; they'd hit rock bottom, and then they surrendered. I wonder if pain, terrible need, is the only path to God."

"What I want to know is," said Robin, "if Mary wants people to believe and pray, why doesn't she just appear on the evening news?"

We both laughed at the image of Our Lady's gorgeous form filling a TV screen.

Then it occurred to me: "But Mary *has* been on the news. They showed her on a bank building in Florida. She's been there for three months. At first they thought the image was formed from the residue of cleaning fluids. But they couldn't wash her off. My mother's girlfriend took a picture and sent it to me. You should see it. Mary's three stories high—she looks like a cubist painting in pastels. Then I heard on the news—they show this stuff all the time in L.A.—that she appeared on a billboard and tied up traffic on the Washington interstate for four hours. She's appearing metaphorically, you know? It's like she's requiring that you have some sort of faith to believe she's actually there. I think she's saying, 'Remember me? I'm your mother. Pray, be nice to one another. Come. Listen to my son.' But even if they saw Mary, most people wouldn't believe it. There's this C. S. Lewis quote about how a nonbeliever could be swimming in the lake of fire of the apocalypse for all eternity, and for all eternity he'll believe he's in a dream from which he never wakes up. You've heard, 'To a believer there are no questions; to a cynic there are no answers,' right?"

"Wow, Bev." Robin hugged her knees. "You sound like you really believe."

"I do? I don't. I want to, though, I think. I just love the stories. I love Mary. I mean, don't you?"

"Hell, yeah. You know some more stories?"

I had to go to the bathroom and excused myself.

The light in the bathroom flickered harshly a few dozen times before it went on. Then, when it flickered off, I yelled to Robin that the lightbulb had blown. She came in and flicked the switch off, then on, and the light calmly stayed lit.

In the morning, after my shower, I hung the scapular Mrs. Sabatini had given me around my neck, and the lightbulb flickered on and then off again. Was Mary talking metaphorically, the way spirits do? "Come out from the darkness. I will be a light unto you." Was Mary talking to *me*?

I found this intensely scary.

I used to be spooked by my own shadow. When I was nineteen, Ray worked the four-to-twelve shift at the factory and I was alone every night. I was convinced that all night, every night, some man peeked through the gaps left between the shades and the dark windows. I stayed glued to the one chair that could not be seen from outside. I darted from the room when I had to go to the bathroom; I starved rather than risk being watched while going to the refrigerator.

Then, one day, I heard a loud noise and made a dash for the kitchen, grabbed the biggest knife I could find. With my heart beating so hard I couldn't catch my breath, I slammed my back against the wall beside the back door, the knife over my head like in *Psycho.* I stood there for five minutes and then I grew furious. Why was I standing here like this? What good did being scared do? I made a vow right then: "I will never be scared ever again." And I never was—at least not of robbers or dangerous situations, and I was never scared at movies, either, not even *The Exorcist.* But I could not stop myself from being scared by a sudden gust of wind, or an undulating shadow in a parking lot. It was the unseen—not person, but spirit—that still scared me. I wondered why, at forty-seven years old, when those lights blinked on and off in the bathroom, I was thinking I'd just had a communication from the Divine, and I was as spooked as I'd have been if the devil stood in front of me with fire in his eyes.

Was it fear of that which I cannot know, or loss of control—an illusion, anyway? Fear that if Mary began to communicate with me, my life would never be the same, that all my old habits and the friends I chose and my way of being in the world would change? Fear of acknowledging the neediness that had drawn me to Mary? That people would think of me the way I was thinking of these people in Medjugorje: that I was delusional?

At least at the other apparition sites, I'd been an outsider, dropping in for a one-shot deal. But this time I'm a member, one of the tribe, and there's no getting around it: the tribe's weird. So what does that make me?

It's three in the morning on Apparition Hill in Medjugorje, and the members are not flagging; they're probably charged by the Holy Spirit and will keep praying and singing till dawn. I, on the other hand, have been yawning painfully for half an hour and am freezing. I decide to head back. If I get lost, at least I'll be moving and warm.

The heavy hectic woman from the airport has beaten me to the foot of the hill. I introduce myself, and she tells me her name is Annie. "I hate that." She shakes her head. "I like prayer to be private. I couldn't even hear myself think with all that praying and singing. How long they gonna stay up there listening to each other. Dawn?"

"I would say that's a good bet."

"Hell. Excuse my French."

"Maybe we could get a cab."

"And tell them House Number 2? That Bruce should take responsibility. He should've given us a map. He should notice two of us are missing and come down."

That may have been what happened, because just then we begin to hear Hail Marys and to see flashlights winding toward us down the hill.

❧

The first verse of the Hail Mary was prayed in the year 1000, but it really caught on in the fifteenth century, when the Franciscans and Dominicans began to encourage the illiterate to repeat it over and over as a substitute for more sophisticated prayers. It was called the Psalter of Our Lady, and by the end of the century virtually all Christians recited the prayer. The second verse was added in the sixteenth century.

Today people still fervently pray the Ave Maria all over the world—collectively, fifty million times a day. Most of these Hail Marys are prayed as part of a rosary, a circular string of beads that looks something like a jewel necklace with a cross dangling off a little tail at one end. Rosaries are divided into five decades (or sets of ten Hail Marys), separated by a single bead on which is said an Our Father and a Glory Be. They are actually a bit like worry beads.

To say a complete rosary one must go round the circle three times, fingering the beads, praying, and meditating on one "mystery" per decade. (Mysteries describe the events of the lives of Mary and Jesus, beginning with the Annunciation, through Christ's birth, death, and resurrection, and ending with the Coronation, in which Mary is crowned Queen of Heaven. A complete rosary makes a grand total of 159 Hail Marys— including the three you say at the beginning of each go-round, for faith, hope, and love. But in common practice, once around the beads is sufficient.

The frequent repetition of words, like saying a mantra, can put you into a trancelike state, which helps you be more receptive to God. And rosaries help you keep an accurate tally of how many prayers you've said. Our word for "bead" comes from the Anglo-Saxon word for prayer, "bede," which comes from the word "biddan," to beg. The practice of praying on beads—at first knots on a string—did not start with Christians but with priests in the Middle East, in 500 B.C. In early religions it was believed that the frequent repetition of prayers gave one's petition a better chance of being heard than if you said just one, and Catholics still believe this.

These days people say rosaries in organized groups, in halls and churches and one another's homes to pray, or beg, mightily for world peace. And they pray while they're alone, too. They ask for the prosaic—money and things—but they also implore Mary to heal them physically and spiritually, to help them feel peace, to know love, possess faith, and be close to God.

CHAPTER FOUR

*B*ack in Medjugorje, my roommate, Beatrice, says, "I would get the youngest, prettiest woman for my roommate."

"I'm not young. It's the black velvet skirt and the Harley-Davidson boots." It's true. I'd seen on *Oprah* where they took three definitely middle-aged women, gave them good haircuts and hip clothes, and they dropped fifteen years. "You're prettier than I am."

Her face turns a surprising crimson at my compliment. "That's nice of you to say, but it's not true."

"You're beautiful. I noticed you at the airport. I was trying to guess your age."

"I'm forty-six."

"No kidding. I'm forty-seven."

We grin at each other.

"I have four beautiful sisters. Cheerleaders, queens of the prom. And we're from Texas, so you know the competition was fierce."

"But you're as pretty as that, just chubby."

"My whole life. I gained forty pounds last year, though. I had this cancer thing. Had to take medication. Just put it on."

"You okay?"

"Oh, yes. Thank you. I had to stay home from work for a couple of months. Near the end I was lying on the sofa praying to Mary with my leg up the sofa back; it was the only way I could be comfortable. I'd had a disk condition for years. I was praying, I think for my kids, lying there with my eyes closed, and I felt this shift in my spine, like someone poked me there, and the pain left. It's never come back."

There it was again: pain. It brings people to God; then God relieves pain—or faith in God at least makes pain bearable.

Beatrice and I talk all night. Confess, really. We are in a purgatory of mother guilt. She'd had a career, too, and felt guilty that she hadn't been home enough for her kids. Beatrice had been rejected by a child, her youngest, a rebellious, pregnant teenage daughter, who'd recently made contact after several years.

And Jason, my only child, and I were estranged. Something I never would have imagined could happen, not in a million years. Would we ever find our way back to being the best friends that we'd once been?

Jason broke away when I accepted an invitation to live in a cottage two blocks from the Pacific, after I'd been in Orient five years. The movie of my first book, *Riding in Cars with Boys,* was nearing production after many years. I'd thrived in my little village by the sea and was itching to spread my wings. So I'd put tags on everything I'd bought from other people's houses and hosted my own contents-of-house sale, at which I'd sold virtually everything except for my books and my Marys, which I'd shipped to California UPS.

A few nights before I moved, I had a going-away party and had been directing Jason on how to make the margaritas, where to set up tables, when a young woman, a guest of a friend, came up to me. "I just heard him call you Mom," she said. "Oh, my God. I thought it was so cool—older woman, younger man, and she orders him around. But he's your son? Oh, my God, you don't look old enough!"

"I'm not," I said.

"So cool," she said.

Jason's girlfriend was the D.J., and near midnight Jase and I disco-danced to "Stayin' Alive," from *Saturday Night Fever.* (We'd seen the movie five times when I was a senior at college, and Jason and I had memorized all the dances.) But we weren't in sync. Jason made a V with his fingers and touched under his eyes: "Look in my eyes. Remember? Hold eye contact," which was exactly what I used to tell him to do back when he was nine. Once our eyes locked, he wound me out and reeled me in without a misstep. People applauded, which made us giggle; but then, when the dance was over, Jason wouldn't look in my eyes again.

I must have been determinedly unconscious, because it seems impossible for me not to have made the connection: that Jason was angry at me for leaving. In Orient, I'd finally given him the home he never had. I'd laid down fresh sheets, then placed towels smelling of the outdoors by the beds before he and his friends drove out from the city on Friday nights. When they arrived, we sat down to pastas I'd made with herbs and vegetables I'd harvested from the garden. Mornings I made pancakes with a dash of rye flour to add texture, and sprinkled berries on top. Jason and I and our friends collaborated on fabulous feasts we served on long tables out on the lawn. We read books under trees, played tennis, swam, sat out on the dock.

When I moved, I took that all away. Jason had called me only once the whole year I'd lived in Santa Monica.

I thought distance would be a natural and necessary evolution. Jason was twenty-eight, and we'd been a couple most of his life. We'd both conducted a string of monogamies, and I'd been afraid that the reason we couldn't get close enough to stick with our lovers was because our mother-son connection was too strong. (But was the truth really closer to this: I'd moved away from Jason for the same reason I'd moved away from all my men, because I'd rather be alone with myself, because intimacy scared me?) Whatever my reasons, I was never one to pass up the dramatic gesture, and so had put a whole country between us.

When I'd called Jason from Los Angeles, conversation was like pulling teeth, so I'd stopped calling. When I hadn't called for two months and finally phoned on a Sunday early in spring, Jason announced that he'd broken up with his girlfriend—a young woman I'd been fond of, a woman I know Jason loved. Then he said, "I'm in therapy."

"Jase, honey, that's great." I'd been campaigning for Jason to take another stab at therapy since he'd quit after one session when he was an adolescent, protesting that the therapist had told him he was clay to be molded. "It'll hurt more before you feel better," I told my son. "But it's so worth it. I'm proud of you, Jase. It's really brave."

"I can't get close," he said. "I always break up."

"I know. I do, too."

"As soon as a woman falls in love with me, I get repulsed. . . . It's because of you."

This was what I'd suspected. But then he added, "I can't trust anybody. I never felt safe with you."

A knife in my heart.

"I didn't feel safe with myself," I said after I could breathe.

"Yeah, well. . . ."

Our first New York apartment had been in Little Italy in a building where our women neighbors had been born, raised their children, and never left, old ladies who leaned on pillows on their windowsills, watching our comings and goings. It had felt safe to both Jason and me. Three years later, we moved to a larger place, a roach-infested fifth-floor walk-up on the corner of Twelfth Street and Avenue A. It was a dump, but at least we had our own monkish bedrooms, and I could afford the place. I found out soon after we'd moved in, however, that our slum landlord turned the heat off at midnight every evening, and didn't turn it back on till six the next morning. Jason and I didn't have enough blankets our first year there, and a few times we had to double up to keep warm.

On the bright side, there were also two Polish coffee shops, Leshko's and the Odessa, a few blocks down Avenue

A, where Jase and I could eat half a roasted chicken, mashed potatoes, gravy, and a vegetable for two dollars and fifty cents. St. Mark's Cinema had double features for three dollars, and my imagined friend the crack-house guard, with a meat cleaver in his belt, had a vested interest in keeping the street safe from rapists and thieves, which meant I could walk home from work or a bar even at two in the morning and still feel safe.

I used to fancy that that guard looked after Jason and me, but I doubt that was true. In any case, he wouldn't have been on duty when I came home one Halloween, because it was still daylight. It was 1981, the year I'd turned thirty-one and Jason had turned thirteen. It was our third year in New York, and I'd just slaved eight hours on a rush job at a firm where I usually worked evenings three or four times a week, typing computer code on an ancient word processor as big as a desk. The job only paid six dollars an hour, but I paid myself more by keeping track of my own hours, and often would claim six when I'd worked only three, then spent an hour or two on my own writing—an occasional unfinished short story, or documenting scenes from my real life, writing letters, composing very short poems.

Jason had called me before I'd left work, when he'd come home from school and tried to turn on the TV. "The electricity's off. Did you pay the bill?" he asked on the phone, accusingly. Jason used to say, just to check, "We're more like brother and sister than mother and son, right, Ma?"

"Right, son," I'd say.

He was in a constant fret about money, and whenever I

went to a bar, he expected an accounting of how much money I'd blown.

I told Jason I'd paid the electric bill, then hung up the phone, hoping I wasn't lying—and that the wiring in our tenement building hadn't shorted out. My heart sank as I thought that I should get a real job and properly provide for my child—because I couldn't do it. I wanted to be a writer and I was going to be a writer. I'd never hitchhiked to California, or backpacked through Europe, never seen the sunrise after a night of wanton fun without the sobering weight of knowing my son would wake up soon. I'd sacrificed my youth to motherhood. I would not sacrifice my ambition, too. I nude-modeled for art classes, collected money at Persian-rug auctions, typed, and had the illusion that my days were more or less my own. But I was exhausted all of the time.

Jason called me back in an hour to say the electricity had been turned on, but the effect of the worrisome news, combined with staring at the old-style bright-green computer screen, with brighter-green letters, for eight hours had put me in a snit.

When I walked into the door of our apartment it was five in the afternoon and already getting dark. The garbage was knocked over in my path; the television blaring as always from Jason's room; dirty dishes toppled in the sink; a crusty pan, spills, and a spoon stuck to the stove; and Jason's schoolbooks had been dumped in the tub (there were no counters, and the bathtub was next to the stove). My heart drummed a war dance in my chest; my breath came in spurts. Jason was paid five dollars a week to do the dishes and take down the garbage. If I had to work debilitating jobs to support us, the least Jason could do was some housework. But all my son wanted to do was slouch in front of the TV— like my parents. And I thought I'd escaped from them. I flipped into a rage.

"You didn't take out the garbage?" I screamed, my upper lip curling like a dog's.

"I was gonna," I heard from his room. "I didn't know you'd be home this early."

"Do it *now*. And the dishes, or we're not going to the Halloween parade."

That got him hopping. I stomped to my bedroom past the bust of Mary and baby Jesus on the living-room wall and slammed the door behind me. I lay down on my unmade bed for half an hour, exhausted and not wanting to move. But I'd promised Jason we'd go to the parade. Jason's voice may have begun to crack, but he was still only a kid, and it was Halloween. Other kids didn't have to do housework. Other kids had parents in their forties, who socialized with one another and arranged get-togethers with their kids. Other kids were probably putting on costumes and going to parties. I felt heart-sorry for my son, stuck with a mother like me; and there were periods when I tried to act kind and patient, made mashed potatoes and baked chocolate-chip cookies. I even set a time to play chess every night, and tried to stick to it, but it never lasted very long. I was always so tired, and lazy. If I didn't have to work those mind-dumbing jobs, I'd have more energy to clean the house, and the mess wouldn't weigh on me like a ten-ton truck. Maybe if I had more solitude, more time to write, more fun . . . But I might as well have been saying: Maybe if I met the man in the moon.

I washed my face and put on makeup, then pulled on my only winter coat, a raccoon I'd had for ten years, which had begun to break apart like a glacier in spring, and tried to call gingerly, "Come on, turn off the TV. Time to go."

Jason was at the door, his hands in his parka, his tongue poking at a tooth at the side of his mouth. He'd had a toothache for a week. Next week I'd have enough for the dentist.

"You're not going to wear a hat?" I asked.

"Oh, yeah." He grabbed his sock cap from a peg on the wall and pulled it down over his ears. He'd recently turned thirteen, and fuzz had begun appearing on his upper lip. His eyes were gray-blue, big, and a little sleepy. He really was a very sweet kid.

When we rounded First Avenue onto Fourteenth Street, Jason said, "You're always miserable."

"I am not *always* miserable. . . . Am I?"

"Yes, you are, and I should know. You're grouchy for an hour after you come home. I dread you coming home, Ma."

"Sorry, Jase," I said, meaning it, and incapable of changing my behavior at the same time.

We met up with a few of my friends and huddled together in the bitter windy cold on the curb at Sixth Avenue to watch the parade. Jason's favorite was the group of twenty or so gay guys all dressed as Marilyn Monroe. Afterwards my friends invited me to a party in somebody's loft. I wanted to get drunk, laugh, relax, meet people, so I sent Jason home with my locksmith friend Steve, who lived near us and wasn't going to the party.

No surprise, I was hungover the next day, and wrote for only one hour. Then after I made Jason and myself some spaghetti, I commanded him to get the dishes done before I got home, and a few minutes later on my way to work, I was stopped dead in my tracks.

I was about to cross Twenty-third Street, which I'd crossed hundreds of times, only this time for some reason I forgot it was a two-way street. I looked only one way, stepped onto the road, heard the blare of a horn, turned, and was blinded by car lights coming at me from five feet away. I thought, I'm going to be hit by a car—and was hit by a car. Time turned liquid as my hip hit the fender and I floated through the air. My pants ripped, and one shoe tore from my foot, then I landed on the asphalt, horns blaring and cars skidding around me. I lay in a fetal position, and made my body as small as I could as I very calmly thought, "Now, I'm going to be hit by another car and die."

I didn't think of God, my life didn't flash before my eyes. In my more secular version of shock, the streetlights did a dance in the air above me, the breeze tickled my skin, and the faces that bent over me made me giggle. My foot was already beginning the swelling that wouldn't end until it resembled a football, but I felt no pain. When the cops came, I apologized. "It's my fault, it's my fault. What a moron! I stepped in front of a car." Then I sang "Another One Bites the Dust" as the buildings receded from the back window of the ambulance; and when the words "no insurance" popped into my head, they popped right back out.

Then I lay for hours on a gurney in the emergency room, bantering first with the cops, who'd returned to make a report. One of them snapped the elastic on my panties where they showed through the rip in my 1950s pedal pushers, and I didn't mind. Then I joked with the nurses ("What do you call an idiot who steps in front of a car? . . . . Pancake"); the doctor ("If my foot's broken do I get drugs? Opium? Do hospitals give opium?"); the X-ray technician ("I've been waiting for this all my life: Xerox me").

By dawn the adrenaline had worn off and nothing was funny. I was given the good news that my foot was not broken, just a bit ravaged, and then I hopped, literally, into a cab, grateful for the seven dollars in my pocket, and directed the driver to my address on Twelfth Street and Avenue A. I watched the gray city out the window as I remembered, mortified, laughing with a young woman who'd come into the room where I was waiting in the hospital. She and her husband had been in a boating accident; she'd thrown the boat into reverse by mistake, cutting off his leg and severing his balls. Her husband had handed her his leg before he lifted himself into the boat, his testicles cupped in his hand, trying to keep them in place. I didn't get the sense that the woman had been in love. She was a young, beautiful Puerto Rican woman with rippling black hair and bright coral lipstick, with whom I'd felt simpatico. Her husband was old and owned a furniture store. She'd laughed too and said, "My mother says, 'At least he still has a tongue.'"

This was not funny anymore. This was proof of just how cruel the world could be and how mean a person I was. I pressed my shoulder into the door of my building, then sat on the first dirty step, then the next, all the way up the five flights to my apartment, and my foot began to throb like the bass in that song from the early seventies, "D.O.A." I had a prescription to buy painkillers and instructions to purchase crutches; but I had no health insurance to cover anything, no money—except for the fifty dollars I'd saved to bring my son to the dentist—and no idea how the hell I was going to get back to work to pay the rent and feed Jason and me.

Jason was asleep in his room when I let myself in and hopped through the tidied kitchen into the living room. My son had been alone all night and didn't know it. What would have happened to him if I'd died? How would he have even found out? I didn't carry a pocketbook or wallet, or a picture of him. I hung my keys on a chain around my neck, and carried my money in my pocket, like a kid. I'd been in a thirteen-year-long rebellion against my fate and had never grown up.

As I lifted my crippled foot onto the futon, my eyes rested on the bust of the Virgin and Child. I'd bought it for twenty dollars at a thrift store when we'd moved in. Twenty dollars had been a fortune at the time, and I hardly noticed the bust was there. Now, as I sat crippled on the sofa and stared at it, a thought appeared in my mind: I wish I could believe. Then it disappeared just as quickly, as I wondered how I could have spent so much money on such a stupid thing. At the time, I'd thought I was simply imitating the aesthetic of my building, where everyone was from Puerto Rico. The same reason I'd painted the rooms the colors of Easter eggs and cut my hair like Louise Brooks or Cleopatra. I was all about style, and I loved kitsch. I was like kitsch: all surface, out of context, trying desperately to stand out, nothing but show. Mary's image on my wall was a joke, a kitschy reference to an impossibility, an iconic ideal mother I could never be, the type of mother I scoffed at: a passive, sexless, adoring—or weeping, wounded, and suffering—mama.

Mary was the opposite of me. I was more like Eve, the bad girl fooled by a snake, the fallen innocent who'd disobeyed the Father and let loose a Pandora's box of woe. So why wasn't Eve on my wall?

Somewhere under my bed, stored in a cardboard box, was my other Mary: a little silver relief of her holding Jesus, their faces painted flat inside of a three-dimensional silver casing— with my and my ex-boyfriend Nigel's faces pasted on top. Nigel had been my first boyfriend in the city and the nadir of my life. He'd taken pictures of me in lacy panties straddling the blade of a table saw. Then, at an art show at an old S&M bar down on Tenth Avenue, we'd hung that picture next to the disfigured relief of Jesus and Mary. At the opening, someone had written in red lipstick under the diptych, "This Is Insulting to Women."

The comment shook me up. I'd thought of myself as a feminist and hadn't the slightest idea what we'd been trying to say with those pictures. As I hadn't the slightest idea, really, what I'd been trying to say when I'd hung Mary and her Baby on my wall.

I looked at her gazing adoringly at her Son as the radiator

hissed alive and trucks began to rumble down the avenue; then, as I heard Jason move on his bed, I panicked. What was I going to tell him? He would know right away I couldn't go to work. He'd be worried about money. I wouldn't be able to fix his tooth.

I hobbled into bed, my foot throbbing so hard my head pulsed, and hid under the covers. I'd pretend to be sleeping when Jason left for school. I'd figure something out by the time he came home.

The young man who'd hit me had insurance, which reimbursed me for my medical expenses as well as the money I'd have made if I'd been able to work. The near-death experience had been a wake-up call; this isn't the warm-up anymore, this is the ball game, I kept repeating to myself. Holed up in my apartment, I began to write like it would save me. I found a job typing on Wall Street for the same hours but twice the money, and with the writing I'd done while I was recuperating, I applied to the MFA program in writing at Columbia University. I'd have to take out a gigantic loan, but thought it would be worth the gamble—plus, Jason and I would have medical insurance.

At Columbia I wrote only autobiographical stories that confused even me. One such tidbit: On Valentine's Day, while her boyfriend, Martin, waits for her with a bottle of champagne chilling in a bucket, "Mattie" runs into an old flame on the street, checks into a hotel with him and his wife, and participates in a ménage à trois. In workshop, when my teacher and fellow students asked, "Why would she do that?", I had no answer. I had no insight, no wisdom, just incident after tragic incident—so many that it was comic. But I wasn't laughing. There was no understanding my own behavior, and lately, there was no getting out of bed. I went to my job; I went to classes; I forced myself to write sometimes. But the rest of the time I was in bed, picturing hypodermic needles sticking my ass, bricks falling on my head, clubs beating my chest. The world was a cruel place, I was cruel, and I was afraid of myself.

After the workshop at which my ménage à trois story was discussed, we all went across Broadway to the West End Bar to get drunk. We did this every week. We drank through sunset; we drank through dinner. I shared a cab ride home with my teacher, who told me, "You've had a life, Bev. You have material to write about. But you got to be honest, you got to be merciless. You got to say how it really was." He got out in the West Village, and as the cab headed east, I thought about that boyfriend in the story I'd written, the one I'd left in the cold on Valentine's Day: how smart Martin was, how beautiful his slate-blue eyes. I thought about the time he bathed me, kneeling at the side of the tub, his hands cascading warm water over my skin; the apple pancakes he'd made for breakfast; the silky emerald-green bathrobe, a gift for my birthday that we kept hanging on the door in his room.

He couldn't trust me again after that Valentine's Day.

In the backseat of the cab, I doubled over. My chest felt like a vacuum, a sucking hole in the middle of me. I hugged my arms to stop the terrible emptying; I dropped my head to my knees and wailed. The cab stopped at my door, and I stumbled out, choking on my saliva, wobbling up the stairs to bed. Jason was watching TV in his room with the door shut. I called, "'Night, Jase, I'm going to bed," and then didn't get up for sixteen hours. When I finally dragged my- self onto my feet, I called Beth Israel Hospital, four blocks away, and asked if they had a psychiatric clinic.

I was assigned Dr. Sprinkle, a no-talk, all-eye-contact Freudian-in-training. Sitting across from Dr. Sprinkle, twice a week, my demons turned into a chorus that could break windows in a concert hall: life sucks, love hurts, watch out, beware, don't trust, everyone's out for themselves, on the other side of every corner is a pitfall.

As I burrowed deeper into despair, Jason tripped toward adolescence. He came back the next summer after camp, fourteen years old, a foot taller, and a few inches taller than I. We were living in the same tiny apartment, where the walls were as thin as cardboard and our beds as close as a whisper. Without consciously making the decision, I gave up men for five years, because I didn't trust myself with them, and because I needed to make room for the man my son would grow into.

I wore black all through my thirties; and one day, remark- ably, Dr. Sprinkle, my no-talk shrink, felt compelled to com- ment on my shoes. "They look like a nun's," he said one afternoon.

They were black leather, laced up the front, had round toes, sturdy heels, and squeaked when I walked. I'd bought them at a secondhand store; I think they *were* a nun's. I confessed that I did fantasize about being a nun sometimes, but it was only a fantasy about wearing the same cool outfit every day, and being cloistered away from the world, safe, and man-independent. It was not about anything spiritual. I was not obedient, and did not like following rules, and certainly would never marry a here-in-spirit-only Son of God, born of a virgin, impregnated by a bird.

It did not escape me that I'd become like Mary: a mother who didn't have sex. Born-Again Virgin was what I called myself for laughs.

During those five years in therapy, I found writing-related part-time jobs such as proofreading and copyediting. I published a few short pieces; I made connections. Jason won a scholarship to Wesleyan, and his sophomore year, I published a memoir in the *Village Voice* called "Sons and Lovers: Breaking Up Is Hard to Do." It earned me a contract to write my first book. By then I was thirty-eight, and Jason was twenty.

Before I flew off on the pilgrimage to Medjugorje, I'd laid over in New York for a few days to spend time with my son. Jason hadn't invited me to stay in our old apartment, so I stayed at my friend Robin's.

The one time he did agree to go out with me, we went to dinner at a favorite Italian restaurant and could barely eke out small talk. "So," I said. "How's your pool team doing?"

"Fine."

"You think you'll make the nationals again this year?"

"I don't know."

"Do you practice every day?"

"Sometimes. I don't really want to talk about this."

"Have you seen any good movies lately?"

"Not really."

Afterwards, he raced ahead on the street, making me trot to keep up. Payback for when he was little and I'd done the same to him? Then, instead of escorting me two more blocks to my door, he dropped me on a corner and didn't kiss me goodbye.

I stood on the corner watching him walk away. His hands in his pockets, his coat switching with each step, and his head bent a little to the right: Jason's walk.

I didn't know why it had been so hard for me to ask him what was wrong or why he was so mad at me. But safe now, watching my son walk away, I knew I didn't want to face what he would say. He'll come out of his snit, I thought. Just give him time.

But then I thought, He may never speak to me again. I could lose my child. And I'd deserve to.

❧

Mary's birth and childhood are not mentioned in the Bible. But her life is told in a few of the apocryphal books. These weren't included in the Bible by the Church fathers, who were, obviously, all men.

Like the births of most legendary heroes, Mary's is an auspicious beginning. Mary's parents, Anna and Joachim, pray all their lives for a child and, to their disgrace, are never blessed with one. An old man now and despairing, Joachim goes out to the desert for forty days to pray and ask God why he's been denied what he's begged for all his life; he just wants to understand. Twin angels come to him in the desert and to his wife at home. The angels tell the old couple, "Don't despair. Anna will be given a child."

In gratefulness Joachim dedicates his future child to God.

The child is Mary. And when, at six months old, she walks her first four steps, Anna swoops her up in her arms and vows that her daughter's feet will not touch earth again until she walks into the temple of God.

As her parents promised, three-year-old Mary is given to the priests, and as soon as her feet touch the temple step, she jumps into a little jig, and all of Israel falls in love.

The priests adore Mary, but when she reaches puberty she has to leave; menstrual blood defiles the temple. It is time to push Mary from the nest. In those days celibacy for a woman was not an option, so the head priest sends out word for all widowers to come to the temple so the priest can choose a husband for Mary.

As Joseph stands among the crowd of men, a dove flies from his staff and lands on his head, making it clear to the priests that Joseph is the one.

But Joseph does not want a twelve-year-old bride. He's already had children; he'd become a laughingstock for taking a wife who could be his daughter. But the priest orders him to accept his fate, and Joseph takes Mary to his family, then leaves immediately to return to his carpentry job, probably building at a construction site some miles away.

When Joseph returns and finds Mary pregnant, he accuses her of lying. Mary begs him to believe her, but Joseph can't. He *goes to bed in a fury, not knowing what to do. That night in a dream, Joseph is visited by an angel, who tells him to believe Mary. She is having a child, but she is also still a virgin.*

When a priest drops by and sees how pregnant Mary is, he orders Mary and Joseph to drink the bitter waters of conviction, which will kill them if they are lying. They don't die, and so are feted with a great feast and a grand celebration.

In the Apocrypha Mary does not travel to Bethlehem but has her child in her little house in Nazareth. The midwife who attends the birth runs out of the house in amazement. Even after the child is pulled from her womb, Mary remains a virgin. The midwife's friend Salome refuses to believe her. So the midwife tells her to see for herself: Mary is only twelve years old and a carpenter's wife; she'd never have the guts to refuse Salome. But when Salome puts her hand up Mary's vagina, her hand bursts into flames.

Yes. The Church needed Mary to be a virgin. She was chosen by God, and her womb must be the home of Jesus only. Mary would never have the ecstasy of, and so be defiled by, sex. Her ecstasy would be reserved for God. Mary was the original lay nun.

Her womb may have been a walled garden, but it was graced with fertile soil where something new and unexpected could grow; her abiding virginity was a sign that even the impossible is possible with God.

CHAPTER FIVE

*a*t breakfast they announce that English mass at Saint James is at eleven and that community mass will begin at five. Our day is our own, so naturally I go shopping. The air smells sweetly of earth, and the sun lights up the low scrubby trees as I happily he d down our red dirt path toward the church steeple in e distance. I pass cows grazing near a peeling barn; a rooster hops from the top of a fence and chases a few chickens into a vineyard; and in a small garden at the side of a little brick house, the last red peppers of the season hang low on a leafless bush. It is fall, I'm in the country, the fresh air is kissing my skin, and I think how I want to run to the top of a mountain and spin like Julie Andrews in *The Sound of Music.* Then I realize: my hands are not itching. They're still bumpy and peeling and covered with brown scales, but I can't remember them itching since I arrived in Medjugorje. How could I not have noticed? I think it may have happened two nights before, while I slept next to Father Freed on the bus.

As I reach the main road, a bus filled with pilgrims groans

by before I cross to a cafe and sit at an outdoor table. I order a cappuccino and look down the length of the main road, which is lined with restaurants and religious stores, at which shopkeepers are hauling revolving racks of rosaries onto the sidewalks. Not far in the opposite direction are the twin spires of Saint James Church. When we walked through its court-yard last night on our way to Apparition Hill, a group of punky Irish kids sat on their haunches smoking cigarettes and staring at a tall bank of votive candles as though it were a campfire. As I sip my watery cappuccino, I wonder what it would have felt like to visit a place like Medjugorje when I was a teenager. People still harvest their own grapes to make the wine for their tables; they milk cows, gather eggs from their chickens, herd goats. It's easier to experience the sacred when the texture of daily life is so close to nature, when the air smells sweet and the silence is so deep.

But then I overhear some Australians next to me say that two hundred Parisians are making camp at the edge of town, and as I see thirty or so Koreans wearing Day-Glo lime-green scarves hurry by, I wonder if I'm experiencing the spiritual equivalent of an optical illusion. How can the village contain so many foreigners and still feel so quaint and rustic—and impossibly uncrowded? There are Americans and Canadians, but most visitors are European—Spaniards, Italians, Irish, Germans, quite a few of them surprisingly young and beautiful and stylish. The place feels like a small village but with a spark of excitement, like an outdoor music festival is about to happen. You have the sense of there being tourists, but not couples on romantic weekends or small clutches of friends strolling leisurely around. People stroll, but with an air of anticipation, or purpose. Almost everyone dangles rosary beads from their hands, and many wear big crucifixes bouncing on chains or strings of leather against their chests—a style too forbidding for me to take up, but I'm thinking the right rosary beads will make a fine necklace, and I'm eager to take up the hunt.

I love the baby-blue plastic rosary Mrs. Sabatini gave me, but my head is too big to fit through its loop, and I want some beads made of semiprecious stones that will look more like jewels. I pay for my cappuccino with American dollars, then begin combing through the shops, to discover that there are thousands of beads to choose from. As I finger my way through red, blue, pink, purple, amethyst, and clear crystal beads on revolving racks, I'm tempted by a rosary made from crushed rose petals, but finally settle on a string of large, round, faceted stones that refract all the colors of the rainbow and, according to the tag, are called aurora borealis. As I leave the tiny shop I pass three men in military uniforms with rifles slung over their shoulders, who've just climbed out of a UN peacekeeping-force van and are gazing at a row of about twenty foot-high Mary statues. I gaze too, but the Marys are too saccharine, too much like Little Bo Peeps. Somewhere in this village, I know, I will find exactly the right Mary to begin my true statue collection back home, which so far consists of only two beautiful twin (a pink and a blue) Mary candles.

As I string my new rosary beads around my neck, I realize it's well past noon and that I've completely forgotten about, and missed, English mass. But I don't beat myself up about it; the day is too glorious to spend inside, and I can feel God more easily gazing at a mountain than at a crucifix. I head out toward the hills that edge the town and think, What if Mary really is here, and looking down at me this minute? How wonderful it would be to really believe that Mary has taken me under her wing—or folded me into her cape—and has plans for me! And perhaps these would involve the kind of self-knowledge that causes pain, but as a reward or a healing balm, Mary would give me glorious sunny, breezy days like this, a feeling of blessedness. But to have the Holy Mother paying constant attention to me, I'd have to be paying attention to her. Or was it vice versa? Only if I paid attention to, or focused on, Mary would I notice the gifts and communications she was giving to me. This kind of attention, I knew, would require a daily practice of meditation and prayer.

I'd called my old religion professor at Wesleyan when I was doing research for the radio documentary to ask him about prophets and seers. He told me that in Christ's time miracle workers were a dime a dozen and that apocalyptic prophets, forewarning the end of the world, were as old as the Bible itself. Then he told me about a colleague who claims prayer cured him of depression.

I e-mailed this professor and asked him what he means by the word "prayer." He said, "A dialogue with God. It's easier if you can actually picture someone. In my case, it's Jesus. Typically, such a dialogue would begin with 'Show yourself to me,' or simply 'Help me.'"

The person I'd chosen to commune with was Mary. For

the nine months before I'd come to Medjugorje, I'd meditated, picturing her holding me in her lap; sometimes I pictured myself sitting on the floor, leaning into the folds of
her dress. I asked the Blessed Mother to help me. "Please," I
said, "show me the way." I prayed Hail Marys. I memorized
the Memorare, then prayed that too.

And during those nine months, when I was also reporting
for the radio documentary, I'd been given personal messages
from Mary through two different seers.

The first was Gianna Sullivan, a pharmacologist in Mary-
land, who receives a message from Mary every Thursday night
in her local church.

Gianna's spiritual adviser, a priest, had forbidden my producer, David, to use recording equipment. When Gianna
invited us to come anyway to receive a blessing from Our
Lady, we agreed not to record, but on the phone I'd said,
"But if I have an experience that I feel compelled to talk
about, I'll have to include it for the integrity of my work—"

"Do what you feel you must," Gianna had interrupted.
"But I'd imitate Our Lady. Be patient and obedient like she
is. And you won't believe the graces you'll receive."

I hadn't decided whether I'd be patient and obedient or
not, but I did know that David and I had to go get that
blessing. I had to know what a blessing felt like. I wondered
if it would be the same as being under a lucky star.

Right away, I spotted Gianna in the front pew and was put
off by her Catholic-schoolgirl outfit—kelly-green sweater,
white Peter Pan collar, long tartan-plaid pleated skirt. During the apparition she smiled and nodded up at the air where

Mary was supposedly standing, then pulled out a yellow legal pad and took dictation. I just knew she'd been the type of kid who always did her homework, the type who'd tell on you when you knocked her book off her desk as a tiny torture.

Then, when we walked into the room behind the altar to meet with her afterwards, and I observed how she stood so close to her big burly husband she could have been an appendage, I reverted even more to adolescence and felt competitive: Mary talked to Gianna and not to me; Gianna knew how to be obedient and devoted, and so, of course, also how to lean on a man. I'd hated thinking like this, especially when Gianna took both of my hands and said, "Beverly, Our Lady says you are a beautiful person."

"Thank you." I blushed.

"Inside."

Gianna had obviously sensed I'd actually been thinking of the other kind of beauty. Caught in my superficiality, I flushed deeper. Then she added, "Our Lady says your work is just beginning."

In Phoenix, Arizona, I'd sat at the feet of Estella Ruiz as she had her vision. Estella was a mother of seven kids who'd put herself through college at forty years old. She'd received a master's degree, and after all her education she couldn't believe in God anymore. But then one morning on her way to work as a school administrator, Mary appeared in her living room.

"Will you help me, my daughter?" Mary said.

"When you see her, you can't refuse her—no way," Estella explained. "She's so beautiful, so peaceful, you'll do anything she asks." Mary asked Estella to bring her message to the world, and in exchange Mary would help Estella's family. Her youngest son, who was addicted to crack, quit in two weeks.

"Our Lady is very sneaky," Estella said. "That's how she works. She sneaks into your heart."

After the apparition, Estella had seemed a different person. Her face was wet with sweat when she wrapped me in a hug, her voice hot and breathless in my ear. "Our Lady loves you very much. She wants you to believe that with all your heart. And that she has you doing a great work that will bring many people back to God's love. And she thanks you. She thanks you. I thank you."

I'd been so unable to accept the message that it instantly flew from my mind until a few months later, when David played Estella's breathless voice on a tape.

Walking through the countryside in Medjugorje, I consider how Mary did sneak into my heart back in Orient and that maybe she'd been trying to sneak into my heart for decades. And how in a way I had done her work. The documentary had been heard on National Public Radio by millions of people. Wouldn't it be wonderful, I think, as I notice how the shadows of the dappled leaves on the ground have run into one another, if Mary really did say I was beautiful? If I really was beautiful, and not a lump of charcoal, inside?

Suddenly I notice that those shadows I've been staring at have not only run into one another but are awfully long, and I fairly run back to town, afraid of missing mass again.

As I approach Saint James, I see that there's a crowd in the courtyard, and realize it's spilled over from inside the church. I kick myself for not thinking to come an hour early to get a seat as I weave my way through a group of Latin Americans, but get only as far as the vestibule, which I decide is a perfect reflection of my religious commitment: I'm here, but not all the way. I'm still on the outside looking in.

People pray all around me in different languages, which makes a mellifluous babble. After ten minutes, I'm finally able to make out the words (from the Spanish I'd learned when I'd lived in Mexico)—"Santa Maria, madre de Dios," Holy Mary, Mother of God—and realize (duh) they're praying the rosary. So I pull mine from around my neck and add English to the chorus, remembering, as I do, a visual image I have from Mexico. I lived in a little village with Kip, and had been doing dishes at the kitchen window when I noticed that the pink neon cross on top of the village church was in flames. I'd called Kip to come look and we'd watched, amazed, as a small man climbed the steep, slanted roof, then balanced himself as he beat at the flames with his coat. Kip and I had laughed that it was "so Mexico." But I must have experienced the burning cross as a call, because after that I kept thinking, every day when I finished writing, that I should go to that church and check it out. I'd been living in the village three months and never been inside. I hardly ever left our garden walls. I was the only gringa in town, a tall stranger, and everywhere I went, people stared. I knew I should get over this, that I was depriving myself of experiences I might never have again in my life. So one day I finally gathered my courage and walked by the snarling dogs and the staring people to the church.

A service was in progress, and I felt too shy, too much of a trespasser, to take a seat. The priest was kneeling at the altar with his back to the rest of the church, chanting. When he stopped, the women chanted back. The sound echoed and vibrated through me. It was so beautiful I really wanted to sit and stay awhile, but I didn't want to interrupt their service, didn't want to be a foreign distraction. But as they continued chanting back and forth, the pull became too strong, and I sat in the second pew from the back. A moment after I took my seat, the women broke into song, and the woman directly behind me sent shivers down my spine. Her voice was like an angel's, unearthly, as though a choir of birdsong had flown from her throat.

I'd never thought that amazing voice had been a reward for taking a seat in the church, but I do think that now. I also think that if I can force myself to stay in the vestibule with my legs killing me like they are, I may receive some sort of subtle reward—if only from the relief of sitting down. But I can't make myself do it. I leave before the service is over and get a little lost—yet another perfect metaphor to describe my spiritual state.

Dinner consists of veal cutlets along with homemade mashed potatoes, an oily green salad, and carafes of homemade white wine. I sit next to the sisters and show them my new rosary beads, then drink quite a bit. So, it seems, does everyone else. After dinner a woman at the far end of the table raises her glass to "Our Lady," and then we stand one by one and tell how we came to be here. Mrs. Benedetti, the seventy-two-year-old woman with the metal cane whom my roommate, Beatrice, shepherded around, tells how she had a stroke and was flat on her back, praying to the Blessed Mother to give her strength. She promised the Blessed Mother that if she recovered she'd come directly to Medjugorje and climb Mount Krizevac. She pats the half-dollar-sized medal with a relief of Mary that's on her chest and says, "It's two months later and here I am." We all applaud.

Beatrice tells her manager-of-a-bank story. "Our Lady has been calling, but I wasn't ready to hear. Finally, she made it happen, so I had no choice."

The woman across from me felt a calling and became a paramedic. She and her husband drive in a van around rural Virginia, bringing medicine to the indigent. "We live in a shack with a wood stove and plant our own food. When I signed up for this trip I was seventeenth on the waiting list and didn't have any money. I prayed to Our Lady. If she wanted me to come, I'd get here. And here I am." The woman has a huge scapular on her chest, and when I ask what it signifies, she tells me she's a lay Carmelite, which I found out is an order of mendicant nuns dating back to the twelfth century.

The lovely birdlike woman with the melodious praying voice from the night before stands. "I'm Leslie Berman. I'm a psychotherapist in New York. I've led a few groups to Medjugorje. This is my fifth time, and each time I come home richer than when I left. Our Lady is very good. She loves each and every one of us, and there's a reason why she brought us here. Some of us may already know why, and some of us won't know till we get home, or not for years to come. Our Lady is so good, and we're in her heart, so we're good too."

Amens chorus around the table.

Annie, the hectic, angry woman who came down the hill with me the night before, looks a lot less hectic and angry. She's smiling. "I don't have a career. I'm a mother. I have two girls and a wonderful husband, twenty years older than me. He knew I wanted to come, and it's a hardship, but we scraped the money together. I used to be independent, never wanted to get married, but then I changed. My husband wants me to stay home with the girls, and I'm happy. . . . I just want to say that when we got to the airport in Rome, from the beginning really, I was nervous. Calling home, worrying. Mad because it wasn't the way I thought it should be. Then, being here . . . everybody praying the rosary out on the street, and tonight going to the service with all those people, old people on their knees out of love for Our Lady . . . feeling her so near . . . We're all her children, and we all came because we love her. It felt so good. I felt so happy. I just want to apologize for the way I was."

I don't know whether it's the wine or the talk or the air in Medjugorje, but I know I've been feeling some of the euphoria she's talking about. I stand. "Well, I'm forty-seven years old, and the last time I went to church before this last year, I was thirteen." Then I launched into my by-now-rote story of collecting Marys, going to apparitions, wanting more, coming here. Followed by my confession that I may write about this pilgrimage.

"I'm too boring," "We'd better watch out," "Change my name" chime around the table, then trail off into "Our Lady is calling you. She wants you for something. That's the way she is—she's sneaky. She wants you to write a book. Oh, you wait—she'll use you. Talk shows—you'll be on talk shows."

None of us want to leave, so we stay in our seats drinking, and then after one sip of wine too many I cannot restrain myself a moment longer. "What do you think about women priests?" I ask my table neighbors. "Do you think women should be ordained?"

Everyone smiles indulgently. Little Sista Alma thinks they should. "There is no reason why there shouldn't be women priests."

"There never has been. I suppose there's a reason," says Annie.

Diane, the blond daughter of the big-haired mother-daughter fashion-design team from Nashville, pipes up. "It's not feminine to want to lead. We do it our own way."

Not feminine to want to lead? That enrages every feminist bone in my body. "And what way is feminine? Subterfuge? Manipulation? Great, give all the power to men. Let them make all the decisions. Why the hell do you think the world's so screwed up?"

The women said:

"It's not about power."

"You'll find out."

"It's about love."

"And nurturing."

"Women have more important skills."

"Look at Our Lady. Imitate her."

"Who was at the cross when Christ died?" The women. The men fled. The men. Huh! One betrayed him, one denied him, and the rest ran away. Women were with the apostles the whole time. They were in the early Church. For all we know, Jesus thought of them as equals. But it was the men who learned to write, the men who wrote the Bible and chose what writings got in. Who was it who told Jesus to change that water into wine at that wedding so everybody would have a good time? His mother. Jesus didn't even want to do it. I just know what happened after the Resurrection. Mary rounded all those apostles together and told them, 'Stop hiding like sniveling little cowards and snap to it; we've got work to do.' Look who's on this pilgrimage: women. Oh—and the 'infallible' Pope: what does he think, the earth can sustain everyone's having seventeen babies? The Church is so hypocritical. Divorce is a mortal sin, and if you're poor you rot in hell for remarrying, but if you have enough money the Church grants you an annulment? They can change dogma when it's convenient—or profitable."

"Some of the biggest converts were the biggest sinners," someone interrupts; I think she's talking about me and am flattered.

"Our Lady will use you."

"Is your name-saint Theresa?" the lay Carmelite nun asks me. She's been sitting there grinning and enjoying the debate. I'd had a feeling she might be simpatico but too politic or bemused to take on the crowd. "Who's your name-saint?" she asks.

"I don't know."

"Therese," she says. "Therese, the Little Flower. You remind me of her."

"I'd love to be named Therese."

"A Carmelite. Maybe you'll be a Carmelite. Are you married?"

"No. Divorced. But he's dead now. I'm a widow." Ray had died a few months before. Jason and I had gone to his funeral, and this was the first time it had occurred to me to refer to myself as a widow. Maybe Mary had paved the way for me to join the life of a "religious": "That means I could be a nun, right?"

"It depends on what you're called to do. Carmelites hear a calling."

I wonder what that would sound like.

"You guys all just follow whatever the Pope says?" I can't let it go, even as I try not to judge them for their blind obedience.

They nod.

"You believe it's a sin to use birth control?"

They nod.

"And you believe masturbation is a sin?"

"Oooh, Beverly!"

Back in our bedroom, Beatrice presents me with a gift: a foot-tall, white, pressed-marble statue of the Virgin as she's depicted in Medjugorje, walking on a swirl of clouds, looking downward, one hand stretched out and her cape flying behind.

"Oh, Beatrice," I say, "it's so beautiful! You're so generous." She's brought an empty suitcase to fill with gifts for people, and plans to give away all her clothes so she can fill her other suitcase too. In one day, she's already bought hundreds of Mary medals, plastic rosary beads, prayer cards to pass out to people back home. The nuns in her town will get one of everything she's bought, and Beatrice will pass a medal to each woman at her bingo game—which she has volunteered to run every Friday evening for the past fifteen years.

The statue is beautiful, heavy, and feels smooth and cool as I run my hand over it.

"Look." Beatrice takes it from me. "This one's unusual. They're hard to find. She's crying."

There is a shiny track and a tear on her left cheek.

I kiss it.

❦

Mary is mentioned more times in the Koran than she is in the Bible. In fact, the Koran paints a more vivid picture of Mary than of Jesus, who isn't the Son of God, but he is the Chosen One, the Messiah.

Mary is all alone, a single mother, when she gives birth to Jesus. On the ground, leaning against a date palm tree, she says, "Would that I had died before this and become a thing forgotten, unremembered."

Mary's pain in childbirth isn't mentioned in the Bible, but we see clearly the pain she felt as a mother.

When Christ is eight days old, Mary and Joseph bring him to the temple to dedicate him to God, as all firstborn male children of the Jewish faith must be. There, the holy man Simeon prophesies to Mary, "A sword shall pierce through thy soul also, that the thoughts of many hearts may be revealed." Mary will be wounded with the pain of mother love: her pain will help others reveal the secrets in their own hearts; then her love will flow and flow, pouring graces over us all.

Then, when Jesus is twelve, he and Mary and Joseph go to Jerusalem with a group of friends and family to celebrate the Passover feast. On their way back home, the party travels a full day before they realize they'd left Jesus behind. When Joseph and Mary return to Jerusalem to look for him, it takes three days before they find him—in the temple, asking and listening and answering questions, like Plato.

Mary says, "Child, why have you treated us like this? Look, your father and I have been searching for you in great anxiety."

Jesus responds, "Why are you searching for me? Did you not know I would be in my Father's house?"

They return home, where Jesus is obedient to them, and "his mother treasured all these things in her heart."

Many years pass; Jesus is near thirty, and Joseph is no longer in the picture. Jesus has been baptized by John the Baptist and has begun to gather his disciples, but he has not yet preached or performed any miracles in public. He and his mother and the apostles attend a wedding in Cana, and when the party runs out of wine, Mary wants to help. She says to her son, "They have no wine."

Jesus says to his mother, "Woman, what concern of that is to you and to me? My time has not yet come."

Mary basically ignores him and says to the servants, "Do whatever he tells you."

Jesus obeys his mother and tells the servants to fill six jugs with water, then take to them to the governor, the ruler of the feast.

When the governor tastes the water, he knows that it has been turned to wine. And the Bible says, "Jesus did this, the first of his signs, in Cana in Galilee, and revealed his glory, and his disciples believed in him."

The Bible doesn't say "thanks to Mary." But it's implied by the story. Mary is a good Jewish mother, who knows that wine is spirit too; she also knows from living with her son the miracles he is capable of performing, and she knows that contrary to what her son believes, his time has indeed come. So Mary, like any mother who knows what's best, tells her son what to do.

Mary never minds her own business. Mary did in Cana what she has continued to do all along: interceded on behalf of the people to her son.

Mary was such a strong woman, Jesus was probably tired of her telling him what to do; he had to break away from her to come into his own. Which he obviously did, because a while later, Mary showed up at a door behind which Jesus was speaking to a crowd. When someone yelled to him that his mother and brothers (perhaps Joseph's sons) were at the door and wanted to speak to him, Jesus said, "Who is my mother and who are my brothers?" Then he pointed to his disciples and said, "Here are my mother and brothers! For whoever does the will of my father in heaven is my brother and sister and mother."

Jesus was making a sound point: that the spirit transcends your earthly family; his mission was more important than his mother's feelings—a point Mary no doubt would have appreciated. But the rebuff probably smarted.

In the Gospel According to John, we meet Mary one more time in Christ's lifetime: at the foot of the cross. When Jesus looks down and sees Mary standing next to "the disciple whom he loved" (John, the writer of this passage), he says to his mother, "'Woman, here is your son.' Then he says to the disciple, 'Here is your mother.'" He drinks vinegar and hyssop and says, "'It is finished.' Then he bowed his head and gave up the spirit."

And so the last thing Christ did before he left this earth was to make sure his mother was taken care of and that the apostle he loved was taken care of, too. The apostle represented the future church and so Mary would be the mother of that church. Jesus had ensured that Mary would be around to keep his apostles straight.

And so we see Mary, for the last time, praying with the apostles, who "were constantly devoting themselves to prayer, together with certain women, including Mary the mother of Jesus, as well as his brothers. . . . When the day of Pentecost had come, they were all together in one place. And suddenly from heaven there came a sound like the rush of a violent wind, and it filled the entire house where they were sitting. Divided tongues, as of fire, appeared among them and a tongue rested on each of them. All of them were filled with the Holy Spirit. . . ."

In Jesus's lifetime his apostles were always walking around "amazed" at what he did, which annoyed Jesus, because if the apostles had stronger faith, nothing Jesus did could surprise them.

But nothing Jesus did surprised his mother.

CHAPTER SIX

$\mathcal{T}$he next night I make sure I'm at the rosary mass an hour early, and find a seat next to an ancient peasant woman the size of a ten-year-old girl. Her knuckles are gnarled and swollen and her rosary is clutched in fingers that slant in one direction. Two skinny white braids fall down her back from under a black shawl draped over her head. As the crowd files in, we squeeze in closer, and the old woman turns and smiles up at me. I am one of thousands of strangers crowding her church, sometimes, I'm sure, leaving her without a seat, and yet here she is welcoming me. We're all there for Mary. Some have brought little collapsible seats to set in the aisle, but most stand, sit, or kneel on the stone floor. The space between the first rows and the altar is jammed. People spill out the door and into the courtyard. No one chats; the air is electric; and when the rosary begins, the songs boom between each decade, a cacophony of voices praying and singing the same words in different languages to Mary, our mother.

The atmosphere has the intense burn of a rock concert

combined, impossibly, with the tranquillity of a gurgling stream. The incense is pungent; the candles flicker; and as my insides feel all lit up and glowy, I realize this sensation I'm having feels like love.

I bump shoulders with Annie as we walk back home together. "Don't feel bad," she says. "We were all where you are. I thought the same about women priests when I was younger."

"Thanks." I'm touched by her generosity. "But you always had faith?"

"Yes. I was given that gift. But you will know. Jesus will enter you and you'll know."

Back at the house, I go into my room and feel so safe and loved that my edges melt, the tension pours out, and I weep, thinking of my parents. A few years ago, my cousin died of lung cancer, and on our way through the cemetery to bury him, my parents pointed out the car window: "Look, there's Mary Devito"—my father's aunt. "There's Franny Vansky"— my mother's good friend. "The shiny stone over there . . . see it? Uncle Red." And as we rounded a bend, they pointed to a large stone near the road and said, "That's ours."

"Yours? You bought a headstone? A grave?"

"We didn't want you kids to have to worry," said my father.

"Your father's on one side. I'm on the other." They would share the same headstone and lie in opposite directions, head to head, probably to save money.

I cry harder in Medjugorje feeling my parents' essence, their kindness: my father hammering in the basement, building things; my mother sipping coffee and smoking in the kitchen, the sweet aroma from a pie in the oven, the floor shiny from waxing. Good, loving, hardworking people, who had sacrificed so much for me, for their kids. Why had I never let them know I appreciated this? All they ever did was give. Even now, when I visit, my mother tries to give me the sneakers off her feet, the new sweater she just bought that would go so nice with my skirt. I can't leave without taking a piece of cake, a container of leftovers. For twenty years my father has waited at train stations and ferry terminals, arriving a half hour early, to pick me up. He gives me relish he makes from his garden, afghans he's crocheted; and lawn ornaments and birdhouses he's built and painted, which have dotted my lawns and hung in my trees.

I've been given so much and am selfish, while my parents received so little and offer the shirts off their backs. When my mother's mother died, her family blew apart like a pile of leaves. My mother had landed with an aunt who had two children of her own, whom she made no secret about preferring. My mother did housework while her cousins played. As soon as she was old enough to quit school, she got a job and left, living in an attic of a married friend, helping her with her children while her husband was away at war.

When she married, my mother had hoped her husband's mother would replace the mother she'd lost. But she was stuck with Philomena, who referred to herself in the third person and liked to remind you, lest you forget, "Grammy doesn't get along with people; she likes to be left alone. She was born with a bad disposition; Grammy's natured that way."

When I was a kid my mother would burn with resentment after we'd brought my grandmother a quart of milk or dropped her off after ferrying her around to the doctor and the pharmacist and the grocery store. "Me, me, me. Thinks she's the only one with aches and pains." My mother would whack the blinker as we turned onto Colony Road. "Think she'd call and ask *me* if I needed something? Never in a million years. If *my* mother were alive, things would be different."

The final insult came when my grandmother began to fall down, and even though she gave my father ulcers and made my mother's blood boil, my parents offered to build her a room so she could move in and they could take care of her.

My grandmother demurred. "A woman belongs with her daughters. A woman's daughters should take her in." Meaning, of course, that my mother did not rate as a daughter. And when Philomena's three real daughters failed to invite her to live in their houses, my grandmother checked into a nursing home and threatened to take poison.

Philomena, like me, had been a teenage mother, and because she felt like she'd been robbed of so much, she never gave anything. She'd been a beauty, the life of the party; but the father of her unborn child fled to the First World War, and she was forced to marry Big Mike Donofrio, a marriage arranged by her mother. Philomena never loved Mike, and he knew it. He was a bootlegger and a brawler, jealous of any man who came near his beautiful wife, whom he considered he had a God-given right to control. But I suspect that like me, Philomena had a problem with the word "obey." I have heard rumors about my grandmother and a handsome housepainter from Puerto Rico, a rich Jew who gave her jewels; I've heard of afternoons spent sipping highballs at the Moose Club, alone.

Philomena had four children, and even though she was a devout Catholic, she divorced Mike and remarried, then continued to receive Holy Communion every Sunday with impunity. When I was a kid, Philomena still had her hair done at the beauty parlor every week, wore red nail polish and a mink stole, and never once invited any of her children or their families to Christmas dinner, or Easter, or Thanksgiving, or anyone's birthday. She did, however, invite me on occasion to accompany her to mass, for which I was and still am grateful. She led me to the statue of Mary, where I sat next to my grandmother, fingering through the pages of her missal, pulling out holy cards to look at the gorgeous pictures.

Mike died when I was an infant, and Philomena was left his property, which included a house with two apartments. When I was four years old the house my parents rented was sold and we were evicted. My mother was convinced beyond reason that she would lose her second family just as she'd lost her first, and that we'd all end up in the poorhouse. She could not eat and shrank to ninety pounds; she screamed bloody murder at the slam of a door, cried constantly for her dead mother, and warned me over and over, "You don't know what it's like when your mother dies, you're nothing, you're nobody, you wish you could die too."

My father delivered soda from a truck and sometimes worked at his friend's gas station. My parents had little money, and when my father approached his mother to ask if she'd rent us one of her apartments, she refused him, saying, "I don't rent to families with children."

I knew the story and I clearly saw my grandmother's selfishness, her troublemaking, her meanness, but I still liked her. My grandfather was a hot-blooded Italian from the old country. He'd slapped Philomena around, so she left him; for a woman of her culture and generation, leaving took guts. I admired her for ignoring the Church's rules and continuing to take communion. Once, when I asked her why she never remarried after her second husband, she said, "Ech. Who wants to iron pants? You can have it. And why don't *you* get remarried?"

"Never found anyone who could dance good enough," I answered, only half facetiously.

"I always knew you were smart."

My picture was the only photo of a granddaughter she'd hung on her nursing-room wall. And ever since I was little, she'd promised to leave me her engagement ring when she died.

One Christmas, when I was maybe thirty-five and Grammy was eighty-five, I picked her up at the nursing home to bring her to my parents' for Christmas Eve. My mother was frying smelts in the electric frying pan at the kitchen table, and tins of Christmas cookies she had been baking for a week were stacked on top of the hutch my father had built. My mother kissed Grammy on the cheek; then I walked her into the bedroom to help her off with her coat.

We sat at the table and had coffee, and my grandmother

told us how her oldest grandson, Timmy, had stopped by the nursing home to invite her to Christmas. "I didn't want to go," Grammy said. "And he says, 'But Grammy, I don't want you to be alone on Christmas.'"

My mother's chest filled and tightened. "What do you mean, nowhere to go on Christmas? You knew you were coming here."

"Nobody asked me." Grammy shrugged.

My father, who'd been standing in the doorway, closed his eyes and shook his head. My mother took the bait. "*We* asked you. You know that. Letting everybody think we don't invite you here . . . that we'd let you stay alone on Christmas . . . ! See?" My mother turned to me. "This is what she does. Drives me crazy. Where have you been every Christmas for the past fifteen years?" she yelled at my grandmother, who was hard of hearing but not that hard.

There was a smile on Philomena's face.

After Christmas dinner, the next day, I sat next to Grammy on the sofa and held her hand. She said, "I've been thinking; I'm going to leave my diamond to Janet," my younger sister. "You don't think she'll hock it, do you?"

I didn't take the bait. Later my father took me aside and said, "Don't worry. You're getting that ring."

But then, a few months later, I found a box in my parents' basement where my father had stored the jewelry my grandmother didn't take with her to the nursing home. In it I found a beautiful thin wedding band delicately engraved with tiny roses. It fit, so I took it—or perhaps "stole" is the word.

The next year, when I came home from New York for Easter, I decided on Good Friday I was going to visit my grandmother at the nursing home and fess up about stealing her ring.

I heard a faint snoring before I walked in her door and felt a little panicked. Grammy was lying propped on her pillows, her eyes closed and her mouth open, in a deep sleep. I'd been told by the nurse at the desk that if I found her sleeping I should wake her up, because she was due to take her medications in half an hour anyway. I sat on the edge of her bed and watched my grandmother. The closeness of this, the intimacy, made me want to run away. Her white hair framed her face in ringlets. She was wearing a pink nightgown and hadn't taken off her pearl necklace and earrings. I could see the crevice where her breasts began. I marveled at how smooth and clear, how beautiful, her skin still was. Her face, almost like a man's now, could have been a Roman bust: big eyes, straight nose, strong chin.

This was my grandmother, who used to take me to church. She was old and would die soon. To awaken her seemed unbearably intimate. I took a deep breath and touched her upper arm. She sprang up like a ventriloquist's dummy, but her eyes would not open. They looked like a cat's, like shrunken almonds. "Who? Who?" she said. "Oh, Beverly . . . it's you. Oh. When did you get in?"

"A few hours ago." I knew it would make her feel good to know I'd come directly to her. "So, how you doing, Gram?"

"Oh, my legs. I have to use that damned cane wherever I go. I hate it here. Grammy loves your letters. She's sorry she doesn't write back, but Grammy's got nothing to say. Nothing ever happens. Grammy's so miserable. She prays the good Lord will take her, but he doesn't listen. . . ."

This could go on forever. I changed the subject to the stolen ring on my finger. I was not being noble. This was my reasoning: if I told her about the ring, it wouldn't be stolen anymore, and I was planning on her being forced to give it to me. "Look, Gram," I said, offering her my hand so she could look. "It's your ring. I found it in your jewelry box."

"Oh, my ring," she said. "I forgot all about it. It was from your father's father. Let me see." She did not pull my hand closer, but expected me to take the ring off and hand it to her.

I did not want to do this, because I knew my grandmother and was sure she wouldn't give it back. But I had no choice.

"Oh, it fits," she said as she slipped it onto her finger. "You can't wear it. You're not married."

"I wear it on my right hand. See? I use it to hold on this ring." It was an amethyst I'd found in a thrift store, very cheap because its band was so wide and misshapen. "Look, Gram, I'll show you." I held out my hand for my grandmother to return the ring, but she wasn't budging. She'd Indian-given me her diamond.

"Grammy," I commanded. "Give me the ring." One teenage mother, feeling forever deprived and so forever owed, to another teenage mother feeling exactly the same.

Looking like she was bidding a long-lost friend goodbye, Philomena handed me her ring.

"Thank you, Gram," I said.

"Don't lose it," she said.

I've heard that the second half of your life is the opposite of the first. In the first half, you are the sun as it's rising, the earth growing smaller below you. But in the second half, you are the sun as it's setting, watching the earth grow large as you near it.

I do not want to think of myself as the pinnacle of all things; I do not want to be so self-centered anymore—and I don't want to have to be forced before I can give, like my grandmother. My family, my friends, the people I love are important. I want to come back down to earth, plant my feet firmly on the ground, and be with them.

I picture myself moving into my parents' house to take care of them, running errands, cooking, nursing, pulling up shades to let in the light. My old life would be history. No more eating out almost every night, no more great food in ethnic restaurants. No movie or two or three a week. I see my women friends and their ambitions for careers and relationships, faces and bodies, spin into thin air without me.

It's grown late. I'm in bed with the lights off and Beatrice still hasn't come in. I think I will sleep now but am haunted by a documentary I've seen about Mother Teresa. The cinematographer who lived in my courtyard in Santa Monica had shot the film in 1978 and said that Mother truly believed that when she washed worms off of flesh, or hugged a man who'd been dying so long his skin had begun to stink like rot, she was wiping the wounds of Jesus, she was holding Jesus in her arms and giving him love. I watched the film on video back in LA, and for a few days fantasized about joining Mother's Sisters of Mercy. The sisters were instructed to bring joy through their smiles, because joy was the best medicine. The sisters were never idle even for a moment, unless they were praying, or sleeping (on the floor).

I could not get one sequence from the documentary out of my mind. Mother is sitting at a conference table in Beirut. Bombs are exploding in the distance and she is speaking to a table of men. "I am going to the orphanage tomorrow to rescue the children," she says.

"But Mother," the leader of the men replies, "it's too dangerous. There are bombs out there. I cannot allow it."

"I have prayed to Our Lady, and the bombing will stop."

The man smiles condescendingly. "If the bombing stops, I will personally escort you."

Cut to the next morning. The sun is shining, birds sing, and Mother Teresa rides in a van to the other side to rescue the children.

I asked the cinematographer if it was a cheat, if it was perhaps a few days later or even a month; but she assured me that it was indeed the next morning. The implication being, of course, that Our Lady had cleared the way.

The orphans the nuns rescued had been severely neglected, and most were physically deformed. A nun carried one boy who looked hardly human into a clean white bed. His body was coiled and twisted, his face scrunched like a knot. The sister slipped her arm under his shoulders, then began to touch him all over, running her hand round and round his face, patting his heart, stroking his arms. Slowly, so slowly, the boy's body released then unwound. His eyes opened. He looked up at the nun, and then, with the back of his hand, he touched her.

It had made me cry to see love literally, physically, open a person up. And the memory of it makes me cry again in Medjugorje.

Just then I hear Beatrice walk in. I wipe my eyes and blow my nose as she turns on the light, then opens her purse and hands me a medal, saying, "It came from Padre Pio." Pio was a stigmatist, who would certainly be canonized a saint.

Beatrice tells me how in 1967, a year before Padre Pio died, her friend's mother had passed away. And after her mother's burial, her friend returned to her car, which was parked at the curb in the cemetery, and found Pio waiting in the passenger seat. Beatrice's friend got in the car, and Pio said nothing, blessed her with his hand in the sign of the cross, then disappeared, leaving three medals of the Virgin Mary on her car seat. And now Beatrice has given me one.

How have I deserved such a kind and generous person as Beatrice for my roommate? I've been blessed by having so many generous people in my life, all of my life—and all of my life I've noticed only what I lacked, like my grandmother. She hated the nursing home and had completely forgotten that my parents had offered her their house; Philomena was too determined to believe as she'd always believed: the world is an unkind and very disappointing place.

Like Philomena, I've been refusing to notice what I've been given.

And when I've found out how much I haven't acknowledged, will I ever forgive myself?

❦

Mary's death was never written about, and there is no historical record of it. But legend has it that she never actually died; she experienced her Dormition—a falling to sleep. And as she was about to depart this earth, she summoned all the apostles to her side, even those who were already dead. Doubting Thomas arrived on a cloud.

Then, as Mary breathed her last breath, Jesus came down to pull her up. Her ascent into heaven is called the Assumption.

Paintings depicting the Assumption are among the most beautiful paintings and frescoes in the world. In churches Mary is often floating in the dome above the altar, her eyes longingly or joyfully focused on her destination—heaven. Sometimes she looks compassionately and a little sadly down at us, her children, whom she is leaving.

Once Mary reaches heaven she is crowned Holy Queen, in the Coronation. I have one painting of the Coronation, in which she is depicted standing on top of the world and spreading her heavenly cape, which serves as a backdrop for a chorus of cherubim. At a little distance the painting looks remarkably like a woman's private parts. The world is the clitoris and Mary the top of the vulva, which her cape, the labia, completes. Often her cape is painted hot red, sheltering men and women and children inside it.

But Mary doesn't stay in heaven looking passively down; she is all over the world in her portraits, the first of which were said to have been painted by Saint Luke and were highly prized (as were her veil, hair, milk, nail clippings).

I can almost picture the scene when Luke went to visit the future Queen of Heaven. She told him her stories—which he then included in his infancy narrative—and then patiently sat so he could paint her. She knew she would still have work to do after she died. To put it crassly, she knew she'd have to publicize herself. Pain had stabbed her heart and she'd turned it into compassion for the world.

She had too much compassion to watch her children suffer from above. She would come back down and try to help. She would bring them to the knowledge that love is the only way; she would bring them to her son and his teachings.

And so she appears to us, in dreams and in apparitions, like the concerned mother she is, tirelessly stumping the globe for her son, spreading his message, bringing us back to God.

CHAPTER SEVEN

*T*he next day we are due to move to a large residential center in the afternoon to begin our five-day silent fast. Word has spread that Vicka, one of the visionary children, now in her late twenties, will be giving a talk that morning in her front yard. We all arise at seven-thirty in order to reach her house by eight-thirty. But I am still drained from my crying orgy the night before, and the coffee is weak. I need another cup, so I hang behind, as does Franny, the ex-nun. "I got to let nature take its course. Sharing a bathroom's for the birds. You want a wake-up pill?" she says in a Brooklyn accent, then takes a pill herself.

"Wake-up pill?"

"Yeah. Awake. One of those caffeine pills. You never tried it? You're not going to Vicka's either?"

"I should, but I'm too tired."

"There'll be other chances."

"You sure?"

"No." She laughs.

"You sure don't act like a nun."

"I've been known to fire off my mouth, like you. Gets me in trouble, too."

"Is that why you left the convent?"

"It was 1971. I'm in Chicago. The blues, the pill, and I'm gonna stay in a convent? I was twenty-seven. Been nowhere. Done nothing." She's only fifty-two? I would have bet she was sixty. "I wanted my own apartment and the order gave it to me. Big mistake."

"I get stuck on 'obedient' when I think about being a nun," I say.

"Tell me about it. You Italian?"

"Yeah. You're Irish?" She has sky-blue eyes and a rascal's face.

"Half Irish, half Italian. My father was Italian. Italians ain't good at rules."

I am on my third coffee now and getting antsy. "I'm feeling guilty. I'm going to Vicka's."

"Ah, guilt. The good Lord's ally."

I have no idea where Vicka lives, but I spot three Koreans walking purposefully past our door, so I follow them.

We wind through some lanes, then a vineyard, and end up in front of a large stucco house with a tile roof and brown shutters. There are three baby trees planted in the yard, pink geraniums in pots on the porch. Koreans are lined up at the picket fence while a large group of Irish people completely block the lane behind them.

I stand on a stone wall to get a better view. Not one of my pilgrimage partners is there, so I ask the Irish woman standing next to me if this is Vicka's house, and she says no, it's Mirjana's. I've read that although Mirjana has received all the secrets, Our Lady still appears to her once a month. Mirjana stands on the other side of the picket fence in the middle of her front lawn, wearing a knee-length skirt, a white blouse, and pumps. Her forehead is wide beneath bushy strawberry-blond hair, and her brown eyes seem very dark against her fair complexion. She holds her arms behind her back and smiles pleasantly as she speaks via the translator by her side.

"Do not preach," she says. "Live your life and show by example. Our Lady asks us to fast on Wednesdays and Fridays. Pray the rosary in your home. Make confession every month. There is no man who doesn't need to confess every month. She didn't say anything about women." Mirjana smiles at her own joke.

Then Mirjana explains that each visionary prays for a specific group, and it's up to her to pray for nonbelievers and priests.

I am convinced it was no coincidence that I stepped out the door at the very moment I would see those Koreans, so I'd follow them to the visionary whose mission it is to pray for me. I believe Our Lady has arranged the whole thing, and experience what a child feels who senses her mother's presence, then glances up to indeed find her there, watching her fondly.

"Love the nonbelievers as brothers and sisters," Mirjana says. "They were not so fortunate as you. Pray for them. Don't judge them ever. To Our Lady we are all the same. She chose us six so through us she could say what she wants. She chose all of you, because she invited you. You received a call. You left home and country. Our Lady put this call in her heart for you to come here. While here you must ask Our

Lady why she brought you here. If you listen with your heart, you will know."

People want to know about the secrets, and Mirjana says, "Why ask about secrets? Who knows whether we'll be alive tomorrow."

A man asks Mirjana to describe Our Lady, and she says, "Our Lady is a little taller than I and always wears a gray dress with a white veil. On Christmas and Easter she wears a golden dress. She has long black hair. Blue eyes. She is the most beautiful woman I have ever seen. There is no way to describe the beauty and love that radiate from her. When we were children we asked childish things: 'How can you be so beautiful?' Our Lady answered, 'Because I love. If you want to be beautiful, you must love.'

"I would like to conclude on the rosary. Pray the rosary with your heart. Feel it in your heart. When your mind wanders, leave the rosary and talk to Our Lady. Ask Our Lady to take this distraction away, then pray again."

"Is it Our Lady on that building in Tampa?" a man asks.

"How could I know this? I must go now. Remember, every prayer you say for a nonbeliever wipes the tears from Our Lady's face."

As I gather my luggage to transport it to the retreat house to begin our silent fast, I put my aurora borealis beads into a side pocket of my suitcase. I've decided that since the rosary beads are the most beautiful I've found, I'll give them to my mother. I will pray on them the whole time I am in Medjugorje, which will charge them with good juju, and then the next time I see my mother I'll present them to her. Even though she virtually has never gone to mass, or taken her children, my mother's blue crystal rosary beads hung on her bedpost and she'd prayed a rosary every night when I was a kid. I haven't seen the rosary in many years, and have no idea if she still prays. I decide I'll ask her when I present her with her gift. I'll feel so much better about her dying if I know she feels close to Mary.

My mother's Mary miracle was the first Mary story I ever heard. When my mother was twelve, her mother died of TB. Her father, an Italian immigrant who dug ditches for a living, could not afford to keep the family together. So my mother and her seven brothers and sisters became wards of the state—and were basically farmed out as child labor. Eventually, my mother was taken in by an aunt and treated like Cinderella.

Six months later, she went swimming in a lake and started to drown. She went under once; she went under twice. Flailing and struggling and calling to her cousins, who thought she was kidding, she went under for a third time, breathed in water, and saw the Blessed Virgin Mary aglow in the sky. Mary smiled and held her arms out to my mother, and my mother wasn't afraid of anything anymore. A few minutes later she awoke on the beach, choking and coughing, saved.

Her Mary sighting sixty-two years ago, powerful as it was, had probably planted the seed for my search for Mary, and so David and I decided to interview my mother for the radio documentary. When I called to tell her we were coming, she said of him, "What a nice boy." We'd interviewed my mother before for a radio piece.

"We're doing a piece about the Virgin Mary, and we want to come interview you about the time she saved you from drowning."

"Mary?" she said. "It wasn't Mary. It was my mother."

"Mom, you said it was Mary."

"No. You think it was Mary because of the bright light."

My memory is not beyond distorting things, especially for dramatic effect, but I clearly remember sitting on the porch swing, listening to my mother tell her miracle story. I remembered wearing my first two-piece at Lake Compounce, where my mother almost drowned, and scanning the sky for the Virgin Mary.

It was interesting that Mary and my mother's mother had merged into the same person in my mother's mind. My mother's mother had just died, and what my mother had needed most in the world was to have her mother back. It was no surprise really that Mary and mother would be interchangeable; they answered the same needs: for comfort, warmth, unconditional acceptance, love.

It was more than a little disturbing, though, to consider that I might have been the one exchanging Mary for mother, forming my personal mythology from a family "miracle" that had never happened.

I wanted to know the real story. David, too, agreed we should continue.

We arrived in Connecticut at four in the afternoon and sat in the living room. The blinds were drawn against the sun, as they always were, which had never ceased to depress me when I lived there. My mother, who ordinarily would be bustling around offering food, asking our plans, urging us to stay to dinner, sat still as a turtle on the couch, looking tired and pale. She suffered from the beginning symptoms of emphysema and had tried to quit but still smoked. She had good days and bad days, and this day was obviously not good. My father was there, too, sitting in his easy chair. He's a shy man, uneasy around strangers and like a cat with his routines, but he seemed genuinely happy to see us and stood to kiss me on the cheek and to offer David his hand.

The television gets turned on at around noon at my parents' house and is never shut off until they both go to bed. It's their tranquilizer; but when company arrives, the volume is lowered to a murmur out of politeness. This afternoon, however, a Carmen Miranda movie was on, and the TV stayed cranked at full volume. "I love her," my mother said, shuffling the deck of cards she'd been playing solitaire with.

"Me, too."

"I've been thinking." She jumped right in with the old energy now. "It *was* Mary. You were right."

"Wait," I said. David had to set up the recording equipment, which would take a few minutes, but I couldn't resist. "So why'd you say it was your mother?"

"I don't know. I was confused. I'm old."

David positioned the microphone between us and I asked my mother to tell us her story. "I was swimming with my cousins, splashing and fooling around. When I started to go under, they thought I was kidding. I went down once. I went down twice. I remember I saw the buoy; then I went down for the third time and didn't come back up. And I saw her."

She was seeing her again in the living room; I could tell by her face, which looked twenty years younger. "So beautiful. The light. There's no way to describe it. It's like nothing on this earth. You felt so . . . I don't know . . . good, peaceful. You can't know unless you see it. It was the Virgin Mary. Then I woke up. On the beach. Saved."

"You can't know unless you see it": a little defensiveness in her tone when she said that, an anticipation of a cynical reaction, but strident too, sure now of what she'd seen. The defensiveness would not have been there when I was a child and believed everything my mother said and even subscribed to her exact point of view. My mother had thought I'd go through adolescence and come out the other end of it her best friend. She'd expected that I'd marry and live next door, that my children would run in and out of her house, that she and I would cook the same recipes. When I announced I was going to college, she didn't like it, because she was afraid she'd lose me, and in a way she had. But even though we live in different worlds, I know my mother's heart. And I can imagine hearing this story when I was little and knowing then, too, exactly how my mother felt going under that cold water at Lake Compounce, her cousins, the favored children of the aunt my mother lived with, splashing near, thinking my mother was joking, and the more my mother can't communicate that her terror is real, the more terrified she becomes. She cannot stay afloat although she is a good swimmer. She has lost her nerve. Then she is under for good, and it is dark there, a relief to let herself sink, a comfort to surrender. And that's when she sees the light and in it her Mother Mary, and feels the same as if she's seen her own mother returned from the dead, holding out her arms to lift her.

How can my mother have forgotten this? Instead of walking through her life, expecting every sunny day to turn cloudy, she could have remembered how the Blessed Mother had saved her once and was looking out for her always.

I hope now that my mother remembered how Mary had intervened in her life, that she would see Mary again when she died, see Mary holding her arms out, bathing my mother with love, giving her golden peace.

How alone will I feel when my parents leave this life?

The thought terrified me. This fear, I'm sure, had something to do with my search for faith, begun in the middle of my life, and near the end of my parents'.

David asked my mother to recite the Hail Mary, and in her crackly, wavery smoker's voice she prayed:

> *Hail Mary, full of grace,*
> *The Lord is with thee.*
> *Blessed art thou among women*
> *And blessed is the fruit of thy womb, Jesus.*
>
> *Holy Mary, Mother of God,*
> *Pray for us sinners*
> *Now and at the hour of our death. Amen.*

The sound was as familiar as a nursery rhyme, my mother as lovable as a baby. I took her hand and squeezed it. She squeezed my hand back.

It's believed that Satan was once the leader of the angels but had a falling-out with God over God's decision to produce a son, born of a woman. Satan was furious that a mere human would be above him, the archangel Lucifer, in the heavenly pantheon, and led an insurrection. He lost and was expelled from heaven. Bitter and vindictive and determined to make humanity suffer for his fall from grace, Satan has been in competition with Jesus for souls ever since.

Among Catholics it's believed that because Mary was the human who bore Christ, Satan harbors an especially venomous hatred for the Blessed Virgin. And Mary, because she loves and wants to protect her children—and because she gave birth to goodness and redemption in this world—is at the point guard of the battle against Satan. In paintings, Mary is depicted in front of even the archangel Michael leading a charge of angels against the forces of darkness.

According to legend, Pope Leo XIII, who was subject to visions and auditory messages from heaven, overheard God speaking with Satan at the turn of the twentieth century. Satan said that he was winning more and more souls and in a short time he would win the world. God discharged Mary, his strongest force, to win the decisive battle, and so she appears more and more frequently, ardently imploring her children to pray, because prayer is the absolute weapon against evil, and the rosary will win the war.

CHAPTER EIGHT

*T*his is the schedule tacked to the wall as we enter the door of the newly constructed retreat house, an odd triangular-looking building with three floors of dormitory rooms near the edge of town.

7–8 Group Adoration *[not of one another, but of Jesus in the chapel]*

8–9 Breakfast *[bread and tea, all you can eat]*

9–10 Father Slavko *[lecture by priest with Ph.D. in psychology]*

11–12 Group Adoration

12 Mass

1–2 Lunch *[same menu as breakfast]*

3–4 Father Slavko

5–7:30 Evening rosary and mass at Saint James

8–9 Dinner *[leftovers from breakfast and lunch]*

Next to the schedule is a sign-up sheet for adoration, which means that the exposed heart of Jesus—the host in a gold reliquary—will be in the chapel every minute we're in residence, and since Jesus can never be alone in the room, we've been asked to sign up for hour-long slots to keep him company. We are entering the retreat house on a Monday and will leave the next Saturday. People have signed up for repeat vigils, thinking nothing of committing to three, four, five in the morning, every day.

I'm highly resistant to adoring Jesus and I don't want to sign up at all. Why would I want to adore someone who tortured me in childhood?

Though we never went to mass, I was treated to catechism every Saturday morning, where nuns in wicked-witch skirts told us if we didn't go to visit their beloved Jesus every Sunday, we'd be sent straight to hell: do not pass go, burn for all eternity. God the Father; Jesus the Son; and the Holy Spirit, who- or whatever that was, were all the same person, and the Three-in-One sat in judgment and would point their finger, sending you far below, where your blood would boil, your veins turn to rivers of fire, and no matter how ardently you begged and screamed and prayed for forgiveness, it would be too late—mercy would not rain.

But if you were lucky—had been to mass before you died, say, and had not committed any other mortal sins, such as murder, or remarriage after divorce—you went to purgatory, where you still burned and screamed in agony, but only for a couple hundred or thousand years, depending on the nun telling you.

I was a black-and-white kind of dramatic kid, who went through periods of heated prayer and punitive self-scrutiny: "You are bad. You make Mom scream and swear and hate you. You must say ten Our Fathers and ten Hail Marys and walk on the floor barefoot, even though it's the middle of winter and freezing cold." But then I also went through periods of stealing cookies and telling lies to get myself off the hook. If I stubbed my toe, my mother would say smugly, "See? God punished you."

During my saintly periods I'd play holy communion with my brother in the basement, using saltines, and beg my mother to take me to church.

"It's not my fault I don't have a nice coat," she'd say. "You think I can afford a hat? Your father works the swing shift; I'm not going to ask him to drive us to church too. And I don't see God sending me a driver's license." She shivered with disgust. "Damn those money-grubbing Irish priests. They're the ones who should burn in hell. Your poor great-grandmother, God rest her soul, went blind crocheting doilies for their altars, and look at the thanks she got. Too ashamed to go to mass because she didn't have a quarter to drop in the box. You think God approves of that? I say my rosary every night. The Blessed Mother knows."

Sometimes I would sit on the front stoop with my best friend, Linda Cholefsky, and pray rosaries. We never said prayers together; we raced because we were taught that each prayer we said for a dead soul reduced his time in purgatory for a set number of years. And if you released a dead soul from purgatory, when your time came, he'd be positioned in heaven to petition for you.

Although mass was insufferably long and boring, it was always a relief to go. My grandmother and I liked to sit near the Mary statue, and I busied myself before we all stood for the priest's entrance by staring at her. Mary was beautiful, of course, very young and also demure. But that innocent demeanor disguised her bravery and her will. I saw how her foot stomped on that green, tongue-lashing snake. Jesus, on the other hand, was skinny and wearing a diaper, with his head lolling on his chest, making you feel guilty because he died for your sins. But when I stood in line for communion behind my grandmother, my hands clasped at my chest, I'd kneel in front of the priest who'd say "Corpus Christi," then picture that same tortured body of Christ flowing to my soul as the host melted against my palate, dissolving the big black smudges of sin with a twinkle, like in a Mr. Clean commercial. My soul would be left brand-new, pure and white like the holy host itself. I pictured myself a nun lying facedown before an altar, my head shaved and my arms spread like a cross. I was a girl thrown to the lions for the love of God. I would gladly pluck my eyes out like Saint Lucy or be tied to a stake and burned alive like Saint Joan. From now on, I would help without being asked, never answer my mother back, never lie, filch cookies, tease my sister, hate my brother, or wish my father would die so I could watch what I wanted on TV instead of endless droning ball games that nobody cared about but him.

My poor family, at home that moment and not in church with me. I at least would be saved till the next Sunday, but if a tidal wave hit tomorrow, or an atomic bomb, my parents and brother and sisters would burn in flames forever, while I reclined on a fluffy white cloud, an orphan.

This made me feel terribly lonely, and because I never

knew you could ask Mary for things, I used to pray every night to Jesus: "Please, dear Jesus, come sit on my bed." But he never did sit on my bed or whisper in my ear, or make the television stop flipping when I prayed an Our Father hard, my eyes squinched shut, a finger pointing to the telephone wires.

I never received one crumb of comfort from Jesus; instead, I received dark sweaty nights of condemnation for never measuring up.

I do not want to adore him. But I'm trying for once in my life to be open, and obedient, so I sign up for adoration at ten o'clock Thursday evening, hoping I may be ready to sit there by then.

Within twenty-four hours a violent windstorm rips through the village, leaving us without electricity, heat, or hot water for three days. Luckily the stove is gas, so there's no shortage of tea and bread, which the fifty of us eat, three times a day, at two long tables. We try not to stare at one another as we chew, and listen to tapes supplied by Annalena and Bruce, who turn out to be purveyors of some fairly hard-core, scare-tactic Catholic dogma. A deep booming male voice: "RIGHT IS RIGHT. WRONG IS WRONG. TRUTH IS TRUTH. LIES ARE LIES. *YOU* KNOW WHAT IS RIGHT AND YOU KNOW WHAT IS WRONG. IT IS WRONG TO WORSHIP FALSE GODS. MONNNNEEEEY . . . AAAMMMMBIIITTTIOOON . . . YOOOUUURRR OOWWWNNN BODDDIIIEEESSS. GOD SPEAKS THE TRUTH AND SO MUST YOU. IT IS WRONG TO SIT IDLY BY AS MILLIONS OF BABIES ARE MURDERED IN THEIR MOTHERS' WOMBS. THEIR *MOTH-*

ERS' WOMBS. . . . IF YOU DO NOTHING, GOD SEES THIS AND IS
NOT HAPPY. YOU HAVE AN IMPERATIVE BY VIRTUE OF YOUR
BAPTISM TO SPEAK UP, LOUD. . . ."

The speaker's fire-and-brimstone tone is enough to make
me experience this as water torture. But gradually, as the
week passes, during which I'm continually awakened in the
night by the wind screaming like a banshee at my window, I
enter a numb zone, where I chew like a cow on cud, adding
more and more honey to my tea, as though sweetness will
provide an antidote to this limbo state.

Beatrice and I have been assigned a room on the second
floor, but Beatrice sleeps there only one night. The rest she
spends with a blanket and pillow in adoration in the chapel.
I shiver under the covers in my tights and down pants,
which I wear under my velvet skirt, my SS jacket over it all,
a beret on my head and gloves on my hands, which are still
peeling and have begun to reveal raw, quilted flesh dotted
with blood, but still, thank God, do not itch.

Day and night I read the Bible with my flashlight: "Ask
and it will be given you; search, and you will find; knock,
and the door will be opened for you. For everyone who asks
receives, and everyone who searches finds, and for everyone
who knocks, the door will be opened. . . ." And when I can
read no more, I pray the rosary and meditate, picturing
Mary patting my heart, or pulling me up by my hands so she
can hug me and stroke my head. I pray Memorare after
Memorare, begging Mary to teach me how to love, to know
what it is, to feel it in my heart, to teach me how to show it.
I implore her to enter my son's heart to give him the mother

he never had, to heal him. And I pray to the Holy Spirit to enter me so I can make a good confession. I have signed up on another sheet for my first confession in thirty-five years, with Father Freed; I'm determined to have the full experience, to give it a try, see what it feels like. Confession will take place at four-thirty on Thursday afternoon. In rehearsal, lying in my bed to keep warm, I run through a dirty laundry list of my gravest faults: bad mother, selfish, cruel, hard-hearted, hurtful, liar. I can't tell if my stomach hurts because I'm constipated from my diet of bread and tea or because I'm making myself sick with the fear of coming clean.

Will I tell Father Freed about Paul, the sweet young man at Wesleyan who lived above me? He took me to my first Chinese restaurant and then afterwards to see Shakespeare in New Haven. He introduced me to tofu and made vegetarian dishes he carried down the stairs to me. I was repulsed by all his attention and let him discover we were over when I opened my door to his knock and he saw another man warming tortillas on my stove. I heard Paul crying through my ceiling and never climbed the stairs to comfort him or apologize; I barely said hello when we passed on the porch.

I'd heard how Mary had appeared to an ex-convict in Ohio and replayed for him the scenes of his life as though it were a movie. Mary showed him what compassion was when he saw everyone he'd hurt—not through his own eyes, but through theirs. He experienced the physical and emotional pain he'd inflicted on them, feeling in his own heart the same hurt he'd caused in others.

I wonder if I'm producing my own movies in bed in my room, or if Mary's projecting them to me. Reading the Bible is becoming a relief and a distraction. I look forward to mass in the chapel with our little group, and mass at Saint James even more, where I jam in with the whole town, pray and sing with all my heart. But mostly I look forward to being lectured to by Father Slavko, with whom I've fallen in love.

At our Monday-afternoon lecture, he blew into the room and peeled off his brown jacket, pulled back his medieval hood, clasped his hands together at his chest, and looked us over mischievously. He was thin and wiry, in the brown robes of a Franciscan with the rope around the waist. We were all seated at the two long dining tables, waiting. He ran a hand through his short gray hair and grinned, revealing small square teeth with a space between each one. "So, we are fasting." He nodded, smiling around. "It is good to chew many times. Thirty-three. Put some sweetness in the tea if you like.

"Do not fast or pray to be better than others, hey? We have no right to judge. You do it to be closer to God. It is good to do. That's why Our Lady asks it. Wednesdays and Fridays. Fasting helps you appreciate what you have. God gave everything to man and woman. Only one thing he said "Do not touch." A big success for Satan when he focused Eve's eyes from all that she had onto what she was missing. It is the human condition. All conflict begins at the same moment, when I become blind to what I have and see what I don't. We are conditioned to believe we need more to be happy. It's not bad to have more. It's bad when you do not see what you have. A man who lost his leg didn't feel joy when he had it.

"Life has to be more simple. We have so many gifts. If you want peace, open your eyes to what you have around you and say thank you."

Father Slavko prepares a newsletter every week, has written a dozen books, runs an orphanage and an old people's home ("for old orphans"), supervises Sister Vera's home for male junkies and the retreat house, and is the priest in charge of all programs for pilgrims. He sleeps only four hours a night and climbs Mount Krizevac at sunrise every morning. And he prays.

"Prayer changes the man," he says, "man changes the world. Pray three rosaries a day. If you say one Hail Mary, Our Lady would say like a mother, 'That's good. There are 149 more.'"

When asked if Mary speaks of the chastisements in her messages in Medjugorje—the punishments that will be let loose on the world if we don't change—Father Slavko responds, "Our Lady does not preach punishment and destruction if we don't convert. She just urges us to pray. Everyone. Catholic, Protestant, Muslim, Jew. In June 1991 Yugoslavia split. It was exactly ten years to the day after Our Lady's first apparition that the first bomb fell. Our Lady appeared that day crying with the cross, saying, 'Peace, peace, peace.'

"We are carriers of God's peace and joy for the world. 'You are important,' she says. 'Without you I cannot do anything. I need you.' Mary asks us to love with God's love, not with human love. Human: I accept you if you are a good boy. But he cannot be a good boy if he is not accepted. Always a lack of acceptance is the beginning of trouble. Love is the beginning of the healing. God loves everybody. God invests his love within us. He loves, not because we are good: he creates the condition that we can be good.

"There are three surprises in heaven: you find people you sent to hell, you do not find angels, you are there.

"Our Lady sees you're good even if it is small, and she appreciates it. The sin begins where thanksgiving is missing."

It makes perfect sense. It sounds so Eastern. If you are focused on what you don't have, you are in a constant state of craving. It's the same as seeing the glass as half-empty. You see what you don't have instead of what you have.

When I was in Orient I'd gone for a weekend meditation retreat in the Hudson River Valley. The retreat was led by a lovely Hindu monk in a bright orange sari, who looked twenty but could have been sixty. Bhante sat still as water as he smilingly instructed us on different meditation techniques, which we practiced in a large circular room with windows all around. We chanted. We did walking meditation, sitting meditation, yoga. And we discussed things. The monk asked what we mean when we say we want to be more spiritual. "What does 'spiritual' mean?"

"It's a feeling. Of well-being," a bald man with an earring said.

"It's what you can't know with your senses," a woman with brilliant red hair said.

"A sense of being in touch with a higher power," a woman in a turquoise jogging suit said.

The teacher suggested that that evening we think about what love is, and added that we might like to have the experience of remaining silent for the rest of the weekend. I decided to try it. I had two hours before dinner and sunset and decided to take a walk up a marked mountain trail. The trail was steep, in deep wooded shade, and it was getting chilly, but I could see a slant of sun over to the left, where I hoped the trail would eventually wind. After I'd walked a steep mile in the dark, I grew frustrated and broke away from the path to get to the sun but was blocked by a gigantic rock.

As I neared the two-mile point I realized I still hadn't walked in the sun or been given even one peek at a view. A great oak had fallen across the path, which I wanted to interpret as an omen, or a good excuse, to turn back, but I didn't. I scrambled over it, then continued to climb up and up, never reaching the fading sun or a hint of a view.

At the end of the trail there was a pile of rocks for a marker, but no view and no sun. I couldn't believe there was no payoff to this hike. What could they have been thinking when they designed the trail? Suffer? The path marker had been a sadist, and I'd had enough.

As I was about to turn and head back down, I heard a loud squawk and looked up. There in front of me beyond the pile of stones was a magnificent view of the valley, rolling down below: A red farmhouse, tiny black-and-white cows dotting a meadow, and the sun disappearing in a blaze of magenta behind a distant hill. I sat down on a rock and wept, aware that this was a moment when God was speaking to me.

I had assumed the worst. I'd been suspicious and dissatisfied, ignoring the beauty of the forest around me, focused on the sun, which I could not get to. I'd been so angry I'd almost missed the view when I'd finally reached it. I'd done this even though I knew that the journey is everything. Even though I'd caught myself many times before this seeing the glass as half-empty—caught myself and promised not to do it again.

I was the daughter of a mother who believed that the world was so untrustworthy that even the weather had it in for her, who could not, until the end of her life, believe it was really the Virgin Mary she'd seen. I had a grandmother who went to church every day of her life but was incapable of appreciating the good that surrounded her. But maybe I could be the one to do it—to see the sun through the clouds. Maybe when I woke up one morning and the sun was not shining and the wind was howling and I was prevented from doing something grand that I'd planned, I would watch the rain dribble down my window glass and think, "Wonderful; I can snuggle in and read a book."

I lie in bed, wrapped in my clothes like a mummy, shivering under the blankets, the wind not howling so much as screeching, as the days pass without my speaking, as I dream of fresh fruits and vegetables, of all the food I've thrown away, of the meals I could have cooked but never did, of the great conversations I have with my friends, of my family and how ungrateful I've been. I griped about how we never had family vacations growing up, or ate at restaurants, or tossed balls in the backyard. But my father did not have enough money, time, or energy to take us on vacations or to eat in restaurants. After he'd quit the soda truck, he became a cop and worked a swing shift. During the summers, whenever he was not scheduled to work days, he worked a second job, spreading molten tar on driveways. I remembered my mother draping hot towels on his shoulders in the evenings to ease the pain of his aching back.

I remember with shame the meals, with desserts, my mother cooked for us four children, every single night; the baskets of laundry carried up and down the stairs; the five beds she made every single morning; and I think how lucky she must have felt that one Christmas to have found those two Barbies for the price of one, so I could have exactly what my best friend, Linda, had. And how hurt she must have felt when tears filled my eyes as I looked at those two cheap imitation Barbies, then locked myself in my bedroom for the rest of the day.

I had only one child, and I moaned about no fun and too much work. But worst of all, I've been stingy with my love. I was closer to Jason than to anyone else in my life, and I never appreciated him. I was never grateful. A deep well of sadness opened up as I soaked my pillow, praying Hail Mary after Hail Mary, chanting Memorares: "To thee do I cry, before thee I stand, sinful and sorrowful. . . ."

I remember one Sunday when Jason was seven years old. He and I and Joseph—a schoolteacher whom I'd been with for four years and almost married—packed a picnic to go hiking up Sleeping Giant. It was late in the fall and getting colder and we took a steep, windy trail instead of the easier well-worn path. I'd been pleasantly surprised when Jason braved the long hike without a whine or a complaint. I knew it was because he was being brave and acting like a man for Joseph, who'd decided to take Jason on as a son. Joseph had kept a distance until we decided to marry; then he began picking Jason up after school once a week and driving down to the beach to empty his lobster pots. They'd even gone to a cabin in the Maine woods one weekend and shot cans off a stump. As we made our descent down the mountain, it started to pour. We slid in the mud, were soaked through to our skins and chilled. My mother, who was Jason's second mother, would not have approved. But with Joe, I felt more like an adult, like we were a family, and the decision we'd made to climb the mountain under threatening skies had been okay. Jason would survive being chilled.

This new sense of confidence felt good. The experience had been a bonding one. I remember thinking that the three of us might remember this day around the dinner table during some future storm.

It was dark when we got home, but I'd left a light on, and inside it was a warm and cozy autumn night. We dried off and changed our clothes, and the windows steamed as we made homemade pizza. I rolled the dough, Joseph made the sauce, and Jason sliced mushrooms with a sharp knife, a thrill for a seven-year-old. In the living room afterwards, I sat under a lamp in a stuffed chair and read *Middlemarch*, which had been assigned for a class, while Jason and Joseph lay at my feet, drawing the log cabin Joe planned to build us. Smoke curled from the chimney and our happy faces smiled in the windows. I remember the wonderful feeling of contentment and how it turned into fear even as I looked at Jason and Joseph drawing on the floor. Joseph had bought land for the log cabin and begun blasting rock to build the foundation, ten minutes from where we'd both been born. But I was at Wesleyan now, and I didn't want to get married anymore. I wanted the same dream I'd had when I got pregnant: to move to New York City and have an exciting life. The depth of the contentment I'd felt a moment before had turned into a choke hold around my chest. I would not be hemmed in by the boundaries of a family backyard, or stuck reliving my parents' life.

I broke up with Joseph on Memorial Day, and I couldn't make myself tell Jason until a week later. Jason had bathed and changed into his pajamas; I sat on his bed and told him the news.

"I'll never see him again?" Jason looked scared.

I nodded.

"We won't get lobsters? He won't be my dad?"

"I'm sorry, honey."

His face collapsed and he covered it with his pillow, sobbing. I took away the pillow and pulled him to me, feeling his heart beating behind his bony back, trembling with every sob, this little fragile boy whose life was in my untrustworthy hands.

I don't think we ever mentioned Joseph again.

How scary it must have been to depend on someone as undependable as I was.

And then, as if that weren't enough, I'd forced him to live with Nigel.

I'd thought I was special in college. I hung out with Socialists who were impressed that I was a daughter of a cop—a single mother on welfare who'd finagled her way into Wesleyan. I'd thought that New York, like Wesleyan, would open up like an oyster, but it closed like a rotten clam. Nobody was impressed with me; I worked as a secretary. I sat in bars and played Frank Sinatra singing "New York, New York" on the jukebox and told people I was a poet, or I recounted the plots of the novels I was going to write. One humbling afternoon, a guy whom I'd just told I was hoping to make a documentary on popular dance made me wither by saying, "Real artists make art. They don't talk."

I got dolled up one night and went with a friend at two in the morning to Studio 54. It was freezing. I shivered behind the rope as Steve Rubell came out and stood directly in front of me. He looked me up and down, smiled, and lifted the rope to let in someone else.

By my first New York spring, I saw myself as a deluded hick, a desperate, unhip little wannabe—I was ripe for the fall. I believe I made a pact with the devil when I hooked up with Nigel Gunther that spring.

I went to MiLady's, my favorite bar, one Friday night after Jason had taken the train to Connecticut to spend the weekend with my parents, and spotted a man with curly blond hair, silver filigree tips on his boots, and a skull ring on his pinky finger, with which he scanned down the racing odds in the *Daily News*. I sat down at his table and said, "Hi." He had holes in his T-shirt and an intense Rasputin gaze. I thought he was so cool . . . especially when within a few minutes he let me know he was a painter, photographer, computer visionary, and Mensa Society member, a SoHo-Tribeca pioneer who'd recently lived in a storefront and bathed in a fire hydrant—and now lived at the Chelsea Hotel, where Sid or Nancy tried to burn down their room.

On our first date Nigel wore aquamarine mascara and told me he was doing a series of photographs of mannequins in store windows and a performance-art piece for which he would take at least one drink in every bar south of Fourteenth Street, all in one evening. Other women would have run screaming. But despite all evidence to the contrary—his calling me twice an hour all through the day, his showing up with a black eye because somebody whacked him with a beer bottle—I was convinced Nigel would be my guide into the world of hip, interesting people, which had so far shunned me.

And all I had to do was be a little blind, and drunk most of the time, to keep believing this.

When I told Jason we were moving in with Nigel, his eyes bugged out and he dropped onto the daybed in the living room. "Oh, no," he moaned. "He's a creep, Ma. Don't do it."

"Why do you say that?"

"He's weird. He's a show-off. Please, Mom? I don't want to."

"You're jealous."

"You're crazy. He wears makeup."

"You are too straight. You're just like your grandparents."

"And you're too weird."

"Thank you for the compliment."

Nigel insisted I quit my secretarial job. I was a poet; I should write poems, and he would support me. Jason and I moved into a loft Nigel had sublet, and Jason escaped every chance he got, taking Metro North to his grandparents' in Connecticut.

Nigel was very romantic while Jason was away. He bought me a skintight Betsey Johnson black-and-blue, diagonally striped dress, tied a short black silk scarf around my neck, and said, "Just stand there. Don't move." Then he took my picture a dozen different ways and sighed, "Sometimes I think I'll just die." I wore a waxy orange-red lipstick I can still taste, black eyeliner, a slash of rouge, and I wrote short poems: "I wear black and blue / I turn myself into a bruise for you." We never went anywhere without Nigel's introducing me as "This is Beverly, my lover. Isn't she beautiful?" Nigel photographed me walking, talking, thinking, sleeping, making love, eating, drinking, screaming at him. In exchange for our mounting bar tab, Nigel traded close-ups of my blown-up lips puckering next to a hammerhead, which were hung above the bar at Raoul's. Those lips were as close as I ever got to the glamour I craved.

Nigel liked me on display, but he did not like me out of his sight. One night I met my girlfriend Kate for a drink, and when I returned home Nigel had a raging fit, then had a fit every time I tried to slip out again. I had no money for my own apartment. I was a captive; then I was a whore, because unless I wanted to endure a crying, stomping rage, to which Jason was privy through the walls of his room, I had to screw Nigel every morning and every night. Usually I put a pillow over my head during the act, as though my hiding would make me disappear. When I got pregnant, I knew I couldn't go through with having his baby. I could never have a baby with him. So I had an abortion, never thinking about it much, just knowing it was something I had to do.

We moved to an old Dutch row house—really an abandoned reconstruction site—far west on Canal. Jason made friends with two kids who'd just moved to the city from California, named Juano and Amaal. He was always at their house around the corner, hanging out and sleeping over. I got him a shoe-shining kit, and sometimes the three of them would come to my new favorite bar, the Ear Inn, and shine shoes for a dollar, then go play pinball at the Cuban fast-food joint down the block.

I stuck with Nigel for almost a year, until it was spring again. It was a Saturday night and Jason was at his grandparents'. Nigel and I ate dinner; then, at around ten, we went out to the Ear Inn, and there in a corner was a fortune-teller, an attractive middle-aged woman with jet black hair and a red flowered scarf tied on the top of her head, telling fortunes for five dollars. I sat at the table and received another communication from the other side. She rolled three pyramid-shaped dice and said sternly, "Who is the man with light hair and blue eyes?"

"My boyfriend."

"Who is the boy with light hair and blue eyes?"

"My son."

"Leave the man and go to the boy. He's crying in the dark. He needs you."

My stomach clutched and tears sprang to my eyes. Had my need to save Nigel been stronger than my need to save my own son? I'd been in a muck of self-degradation, a haze of drunkenness where Jason existed only as a shadow wavering on the periphery. My poor baby. My anchor, my chain, my sanity.

On our way home, a few blocks from the Ear Inn, I walked a bit ahead of Nigel. When he grabbed my arm to slow me down, I whirled around and yelled, "Get your hands off of me! I'm leaving you!" He grabbed my other arm, and with unnatural strength I broke his hold, and then I ran. I ran until he stopped yelling, "Beverly, don't do this! Come back! I love you! All I ever do is love you . . . !" I ran until I could no longer hear his footsteps, and then I ducked behind the tire of a trailer truck and caught my breath. I was in front of a loading dock, so I climbed onto it and huddled in the corner, and slept.

At dawn I wandered around, then sat on a bench and stared at my dirty fingernails; I touched the motor-oil stains on my pant legs. How had I become this person? When I looked up, I saw people walking into a church. It was Sunday. I walked in too and sat in the back. I realized it must be almost Easter. It was a Protestant church and there were no statues, but the sun shooting through the stained-glass window at the same moment a magnificent organ blasted its first chord filled me with awe and a familiar but long-ago emotion. It felt like something powerful and kind was wrapping me in an embrace and pulling on my heart at the same time. I'd had this feeling before, almost every time I'd stepped into a church. It was as though every dead relative I'd never even met was watching over me, wanting to hear me, as though the air itself was a balm of sympathy. As tears of gratefulness made tracks on my grimy face, I believed I would find some way to leave Nigel. I had to.

When I went back to him that morning, he wept for forgiveness, promised he would change. A week later, he said he would baby-sit Jason, and I could go out with Kate. So I went out.

At the end of the night, Kate and I pulled to the front of the building in a cab. The windows were black and jagged, like punched-in teeth. Glass covered the sidewalk. "My God," Kate gasped.

"Jason's in there." My heart thudded against my ribs. "Call the police."

Nigel was huddled in a corner, crying in the dark. He'd thrown a wrench through the TV. The makeup mirror he'd bought me, with round colored bulbs surrounding the glass, had been stomped to bits. The slides he'd taken of me were strewn all over the floor.

I brushed past him and through the mess without saying a word. I ran up the stairs as he yelled, "Look what you made me do! I'm so sorry. Beverly? Where're you going? Come back." His voice was getting closer. He was following me up the stairs.

Jason jumped out of bed and ran to me.

"Mom! I was so scared. I was afraid you wouldn't come home."

"I'll always come home, Jason. Put on your coat and your shoes."

Nigel was in the room. He grabbed my arm. "What are you doing? You're not leaving."

"The police are on their way. Let go."

"You can't go."

"Jason, run outside. Kate's there."

Jason ran.

Nigel's fingers squeezed my arms so hard they bruised. I tried to breathe deeply so I wouldn't start screaming and flailing and kicking and biting—which would only escalate the craziness. Nigel cried and shook me, saying over and over, "Why are you doing this to me? All I ever do is love you. I love you so much. You can't leave me. Don't leave. . . ."

Luckily the police arrived in minutes. "Take it easy, buddy," one of them said. "Let her go."

I never felt safe with you. . . . My son's words haunted me in Medjugorje as I pictured him up in that room, hearing Nigel stomping around, crying and smashing, glass crashing onto the sidewalk; Jason upstairs with the blanket over his head, wishing and wishing, but not believing I would ever come home.

I never really recovered from that descent into hell, and neither did Jason. We slept on Kate's living-room floor until I'd saved enough for us to move to Avenue A, where I sank into a depression I didn't come out of until Jason was away at college. I was terrified of how low I'd sunk with Nigel, and because I didn't know how I could have ever let such abuse happen, I could never trust that I wouldn't let it happen again.

Jason couldn't, either. I think something broke in us. And it was still broken.

"I'm sorry, I'm sorry . . ." I cry, the blanket over my own head, wishing it never had happened. Wishing I could go back and change things. How could I ever repair the damage? I weep and I pray: "Please, please, dear Mary, be the mother I never was. Heal my son's heart. Mother him. I didn't. I don't. I don't even know how to."

If only Jason were a child now, I could do it over again, I would try harder, I would love him and protect him . . .

I think of paintings of the Assumption, where Mary floats up through the clouds, angels at her feet, the world down below, and up above are God on the left and Jesus on the right, holding his cross, waiting to welcome her. But then there are the other paintings of Mary as Queen of Heaven. After she has floated up, she's crowned queen and sits on a throne or stands on a cloud holding her infant son, Jesus.

The sequence is illogical; it's not linear. If life were like that, I could hold my baby now.

❦

The first recorded apparition of the Blessed Virgin Mary occurred in 270. Since then there have been hundreds, maybe thousands; in this century alone, in a span of less than fifty years, from 1928 to 1971, there were 210. But in all time only ten have been sanctioned by the Church, three of them in this century. It's popularly believed that the Church fosters these spectacles to increase faith and to be able to make shrines at which they can hawk relics, but apparitions have always been imposed from below on the Church authorities, who dread having to deal with them.

The Church's stand is that the word of God is in Scripture, period. Apparitions belong in the realm of private revelation, and it would be preferable to keep them private. It's dangerous to spread words from Mary's mouth, channeled through the mouths of fully fallible (potentially even crazy) humans.

The first apparition sanctioned by the Church occurred in Mexico City, where Mary appeared as the Virgin of Guadalupe. It was 1531. Mexico had been conquered by the Spaniards, and the people were demoralized, ravaged by disease, instantly made to feel oppressed and inferior by the white men who now ruled. Juan Diego, an Indian peasant and recent convert to Catholicism, was walking by a hill, where he saw a beautiful lady calling to him. When he approached her, she told him to please go to the bishop and tell him she would like a cathedral built on this hill in her honor. The hill covered the temple of an Aztec goddess named Tonantzin.

Diego did as the lady asked, but the bishop threw him out. So the lady made beautiful Castilian roses grow all over the hill, then asked Diego to please pick them and place them in his shawl. "Go my son," she said, "and give these to the bishop. This time he'll listen."

Castilian roses were the bishop's favorite flower and did not grow in Mexico. No roses grew in Mexico City in December. When the bishop unwrapped the shawl, he saw not only the roses but an image of the Virgin of Guadalupe on Juan Diego's cape, and was forced to believe the peasant.

When word spread of the miracle, the Mexican people knew their mother had come to save them. She had chosen one of their own people—not a Spaniard—to carry her message to the bishop. And the bishop had been forced to pay him the respect of listening to him. Mary's action reflected her promise in the Magnificat: "He hath put down the mighty from their seats, and exalted them of low degree."

What the Franciscans had been trying to accomplish for a decade happened overnight: an entire nation converted to Catholicism. A basilica was built on the hill, to which millions still walk in pilgrimage every year, many of them on their knees. Juan Diego's shawl has hung in the basilica for over four hundred years; it was made of cactus fiber and should have disintegrated after forty years. It has survived an explosion set off underneath it, gunshots, fire, and acid. Scientific testing was performed in the 1970s, and the scientists concluded that since *it would be impossible to paint such a fine image on such a roughly woven surface, the painting could not be of human origin. When a photo of the Virgin's eyes was blown up, the image of Juan Diego could be seen in her pupils.*

Guadalupe's image decorates every town in Mexico and almost every home. To the people, she is the Virgin Mary with dark skin, affectionately known as La Morena. She is the Mother of Jesus; she is generous and courageous and fiercely loves her children. People ask for favors and promise Guadalupe what they will give in return if the favor is granted. One woman promised that if her infant daughter was cured of a life-threatening disease, she'd carry her daughter all the way to the basilica of Guadalupe, two states and a hundred miles away. The girl was cured, but the woman wasn't able to make the journey until her daughter was ten years old. She carried her daughter and walked for three months to get there, but she fulfilled her promise.

Emblazoned on a banner, the Virgin of Guadalupe led the rebel army into the revolution that won Mexico its independence from Spain. The Mexican people love Mary with such passion that in procession they will explode with loud cries like at a soccer match, "Viva la Virgen! Viva la Virgen!"

CHAPTER NINE

*W*ith all of my past life radiating around my heart, I go to mass at Saint James, I pray Hail Marys with three thousand people, I sing, I kneel, and I weep shamefacedly for who I was, the cruel things I've done, but I weep from relief too. I'm looking into my own face; I'm pointing to my own heart. It's pierced with a dagger. It's bleeding regret, and I'm giving it to Mary. Saturated with her compassion, baptized by that sweet pained expression, I feel love for all the people I've hurt, and I feel love for all the people crowded around me at Saint James, Mary's children. I love all the pilgrims gathered every day in our own little chapel for mass. As a group we sing off-key; half of the people stay kneeling through the whole service; and half of the people say their petitions out loud when Father Freed comes to the part of the liturgy where he says, "Let us pray": "For my aunt who is diagnosed with cancer," let us pray. "That my children come back to God," let us pray. "For the end to abortion," let us pray. "For all the priests and religious," let us pray. I say my petitions in my heart, "Please, dear God, help me heal. Help me love. Heal my son."

I do not, however, love Annalena and Bruce's responses to the complaints of three quarters of our group who are suffering from fever and chills and have broken the silence to complain. When Little Sista says to Annalena after a "meal," "It's a little hard to sleep; there's no heat, and my sister has a fever," a woman standing by says, "Jesus lived in poverty and suffered, and that's the way it is. We should offer up our suffering." When someone else says, "The sewer is backing up into my shower," Annalena says, "Offer it up."

Is this the same as "Shake it off"? I once heard a Little League coach say that to a kid who'd just struck out: "Shake it off." Now that made sense. Don't dwell on the disappointment. Get over it. Move on. You still have a game to play, and worrying about your mistake will jam you up.

But offer it up? Do they believe that your own suffering can be offered up to relieve suffering in the world, as though there's a cosmic accounting of the finite amount of suffering that goes around? Or do they simply mean, be content with whatever you are given? Don't fix something that's broken, like the plumbing in the retreat house?

Before we came into the house, Beatrice presented me with a cotton ball in a Baggie. "You know the girl in Massachusetts, the suffering soul?" The girl had experienced a loss of oxygen to the brain when she was three and had been in a coma for over a decade. Her mother brought her to Medjugorje, and since they returned, several communion wafers had turned to flesh during communion in her bedroom, cures of terminal diseases had been claimed by visitors, and oil bleeding from every statue in her room had been absorbed into cotton balls and given away. The girl would sometimes suffer the same symptoms as the people who came to her for a cure, and was considered a suffering soul, who took on not only the pains of the people who came but the pain of the whole world. "The oil's very powerful," Beatrice had said. "It smells like roses." Which it did.

I take the cotton ball out of the Baggie and hold it to my nose as I try to make sense of it all, shivering in my bed, hungry. When I lived in Mexico, I'd heard drumming coming from the back of a church known as a pilgrimage site for *penitentes.* The church had lurid chipped murals of devils biting flesh and frightfully bloody depictions of Christ. A statue of Jesus leaning on a rod was in the main chapel. I'd been told the rod was the *axis mundi,* the conduit between this world and the unseen world. That was where Mary probably lived; where all the angels and saints and devils lived. Sometimes they broke through to the other side, especially at hot spots like Medjugorje. And sometimes you broke through to them. In the ancient world the division hardly existed.

In the church in Mexico, Christ's face bled tears, his back was a gruesome mat of blood; but his expression wasn't pained so much as worried and hurt for us. I had walked toward the drumming, past a sign that said No Trespassing, and peeked through the crack between the two ancient wooden doors. Men with no shirts wore crowns of thorns and beat their own backs over their shoulders with whips. Now why would they do that? To exhibit their love to God, I guessed. To show him they loved him so much they were willing to make themselves bleed. But does the God Father Slavko talks about believe that his children, whom he loves, should suffer for him like that, to prove their love?

Some suffering is of our own making, and so is our punishment. What you do unto others is done unto you. God doesn't do this; you do it to yourself. Less easy to explain is the suffering you have no control over: natural disasters, accidents, evil done unto you.

The summer after I was hit by the car in New York, I was writing at the dining table overlooking Avenue A and saw something yellow streaming down from the sky. A little girl around two years old in a yellow dress lay on the sidewalk. Women screamed; men made a circle and reached their arms out, but it was as though the girl was a fire and they couldn't touch her. A cop car screeched up and one of the officers wrapped the girl in his jacket and carried her off. A few minutes later the mother appeared on the street, pulling her hair and screaming up at the window her daughter had fallen from.

Back then, when I was thirty-one, I wrote a bad poem blaming Mary and her powerlessness for the girl's death; Mary was a mother, how could she let this happen?

People are maimed and tortured every day. Holocausts happen. I understood now what Father Slavko would say to this: it is people performing atrocities, not God. But how would Slavko explain a baby falling out a window? That death is part of life, that sorrow and pain are what bring you to a need for the comfort of God, and only when you acknowledge your need is there room for God to enter? I already knew from experience that once you feel that God-love inside of you, nothing hurts quite so much anymore.

Still, I cannot begin to explain or to understand how to reconcile the presence of such pain in the midst of the love I'm beginning to feel is at the core of everything, including ourselves.

But it is the martyr element in Catholicism that most troubles me. Historically, for the religion to survive it was necessary to promote the belief that it's better to die than renounce your God. Christ died because he was a political activist, a revolutionary truth teller, and society killed the messenger. Christ was a hero, but I did not for the life of me get the connection between Christ's suffering on the cross and our suffering to find grace.

Mary suffered, and we remember her for that, but it's not what she is most celebrated for. Mary suffers the way all mothers, all people in the world, suffer, and she survived the suffering unembittered by it; she survived it with love. She is not a martyr, and she invites us to find refuge in her heart, that famous heart she wears on her chest, flames bursting out, a dagger piercing it and roses dancing round.

Wednesday we make a side trip to Father Jozo's church, an hour away along winding mountainous roads. I've eaten nothing but a slice of bread and a cup of tea three times a day for three days now. Father Jozo was the priest here when Mary first started appearing in Medjugorje. His translator comes on the bus ride with us and leads us in two rosaries. Between each ten Hail Marys we sing a song that goes, "Come, Holy Spirit. . . ."

As soon as I enter the church, I smell roses. I don't believe it at first, but the scent is strong and does not go away. "You smell roses?" I break silence to ask the sisters. They shake their heads, look significantly at each other, and smile kindly at me.

I want to believe that the roses are Mary's way of letting me know she's here, of giving me support, telling me she appreciates the painful self-examinations I've been putting myself through while shivering in bed, unbathed and starving.

Then, when Father Jozo begins to speak, I think Our Lady has sent me a gift of roses because she does not want me to bolt from his lectern-hammering sermonizing. Father Jozo is a burly, unsmiling man with a balding head and intense dark eyes. "During all time there has never been such a time of grace," says Father Jozo through his translator. "Every day for sixteen years. It is not a miracle that Our Lady comes. It is a miracle that you have come to see her. She is our mother, she must come. But she is not here to make your life smooth. She's here to hold your hand. She was not at Calvary to take away the cross.

"She says, 'Pray, pray, pray. Prepare the soil of your heart.'

"In 1945, Communists walked through the door of this church and the priests were given the choice of dying, or living by renouncing their God. They refused to renounce God and were shot and burned."

"Now," says the translator, "the father will lead us in the Joyful Mysteries."

Another rosary!!! We already said two on the bus ride over.

After we finish, Jozo continues. "You are creating a world without God. Show me a woman who has found contentment or peace from killing her unborn child. A wound remains."

Back on the bus, Beatrice leads yet another rosary—the Sorrowful Mysteries, basically a recounting of the stages of Jesus' "Passion," his persecution and death. I've had enough. Especially when she gets to the Scourging at the Pillar: "Every part of his body was torn and beaten. Imagine how the salt of his tears burned when they entered his open wounds, stinging him like the memory of his betrayal. . . ." I block my ears like a five-year-old.

Back in bed in the middle of the afternoon at the retreat house, I feel sick thinking of my confession to Father Freed the next day. By participating in the rite of confession I will be implying a belief in a priest's authority to act in God's name, on God's behalf. I will be a practicing Catholic, which will place me in obeisance to Father Jozo, to all priests, and to the Pope. I will have to confess my abortion.

I smell roses again, and remember the first time I mourned my unborn baby. I was in Mexico, and in love for the last time. Kip was a veterinarian, nine years younger than me. I'd moved to Mexico with him when he'd taken a job to oversee an aid project. There were roses blooming in our garden that lovely summer evening in 1989 after the rains had come just as the campesinos said they would, on June 24, John the Baptist's day. God was part of everyday life in Mexico. Statues of Mary and Jesus in churches were dressed in real clothes and wigs and paraded around. People set up little altars to the Virgin of Guadalupe in their houses. They set food and candles and flowers before her and asked her for things. Yet the first thing I did when Kip and I moved into our little house in the dairy village was to take Guadalupe's picture down.

I did not know at the time that Guadalupe was the Virgin Mary. I thought she was a Mexican saint, and in the crude images I'd seen of her, she looked like a beetle with spikes. I had, however, found a cloth embroidered with her image, which I draped over my computer when I was done writing for the day. After I'd stashed the printer in the china cabinet, I'd balanced deep-blue candles in the backs of the lime-green lizard candleholders on my desk, which was also our dinner table. Kip would be home any minute, and I wanted the place to be lovely and ordered. I carried some scissors out to the garden and waved to the three women staring over our wall waiting for a glimpse of La Gringa Alta. A rumor had circulated through the village that La Gringa sat *sola* in her kitchen and stared at a television screen with words on it— my computer, which I'd had to smuggle in. The fact that I might enjoy my solitude was hard for most Mexicans to imagine. They had huge extended families of cousins and aunts and uncles and grandparents, all crowded into a couple of houses. A woman my age without her children near was someone to be pitied. Children were your wealth and motherhood a virtue in a country that revered Mary more than any other saint, even—or so it seemed—more than her son. Women in Mexico were not "liberated," in the popular sense, but they were the strength of the family. *Mi hijo* was the endearment used to address their husbands: "my son." In Mexico, in the middle of a nation watched over by Mother Mary, I thought I might like to be a mother again myself. In Mexico, for the first time in my life, I thought I might like to be a wife.

I decided on yellow roses and cut eight blossoms, which I pressed to my face as I walked back inside. I arranged them in an earthenware vase in the middle of the dinner table, then lit the candles. The tamales I'd bought from a woman at the picnic table set outside her door were beginning to give off their sugary fragrance in the oven when I heard a horse on the porch.

Kip was astride him bareback, holding his baseball hat over his heart. "Come on, Bevy, we're going for a ride," he said, his grin so bright it shone through the screen door.

I did not want to go riding on any horse. I hated horses. Their nostrils flare, their eyes dart around, and they're huge and unpredictable. There was no moon out there, it was dark, tamales were in the oven, the table was set. But then I recalled last Saturday night and how I'd wanted to stay home then, too, and what I'd potentially missed. We'd been invited to a Quinceaños celebration, which is a girl's fifteenth birthday, her coming-out party, at which she is dressed in virginal white. I preferred to stay home and work and avoid the frustration of trying to make conversation in Spanish, of which I knew maybe two hundred words, all in the present tense. Kip complained that he was restless. He'd done no physical work that day; dancing would be fun. I compromised by playing checkers with him. When I creamed him in two games straight, he complained that I was too competitive, and said, "This is not relaxing." Then we heard the band at the Quinceaños at the other end of the village strike up again, and Kip said, "Come on, let's go."

"No," I said unequivocally; he could go alone. So he did. A half an hour later Juan, the man who'd dug a patch of garden for me to plant herbs in, knocked at the door and handed me a napkin. On it Kip had written, "Turn off the computer and come NOW." I told Juan to tell Kip I'd be there in a minute. I changed into a dress, feeling a little piqued, but I put on red lipstick and waded through the muddy village in the dark, stepping on rocks, avoiding snarling dogs. When I reached the fiesta, Kip was standing with ten men, all of them grinning and nodding at me, all of them aware of the note he'd sent, and all of them, just ten minutes before, trying to get him to dance with every *sola* woman in the backyard. The band was led by the principal of the school and played traditional Mexican-hat-dance music. Kip and I did our best at dancing and the people smiled and nodded and toasted us, the Americanos who had come to live with them. The host kept handing us rum-and-Cokes. When we were all good and drunk the band switched to rock and roll, and Kip and I danced so wildly, people made a circle around us to watch.

I reminded myself that I would have missed a good time had I stayed home that night, that I should try to look at life as an adventure instead of as a problem to be solved.

"Come on," Kip called through the door. "Climb the rail and hop on." I was afraid of that flare-eyed horse, but didn't want to admit it. I stood on the porch rail as Kip patted my seat in front of him on the horse.

So I did it. I climbed on and tangled my hands in the horse's mane as Kip wrapped my waist with one arm and gave a giddyap with the other. We rode through the village, the horse's hooves clomping on the stones, its back rocking rhythmically beneath us, until we reached an alfalfa field at the edge of town and the horse took off. Kip held me close as I laughed so hard from terror and the thrill of it that I almost fell off. Then Kip lifted me off in the alfalfa, and while the horse ate his heartful nearby, we made love on the soft grasses.

That night I dreamed of Joseph, the man to whom I'd been engaged when I was twenty-five. Angry and bitter because I broke off the engagement for my "bigger" plans, he was holding a hat filled with three kittens and offering them to me. In the dream I wished he would forgive me—and then was awakened in real life by a bell at the gate. Kip pulled on his jeans to answer it, then came back to the bedroom. It was a farmer with a sick cow, and he was waiting for Kip outside. Kip changed into his jumpsuit, then kissed me goodbye, saying he'd try to bring home fresh milk, which the villagers sometimes presented him in payment.

I made oatmeal and fed the leftovers to the three wild kit-

tens—my little friends in the backyard. I made no associa-
tion of these kittens with the kittens in the dream about
Joseph. Their mother, a feral cat I'd named May, had delivered them in the stones of our back wall. Neither May nor
her kittens would let me get near, so I'd watched their frol-
icking from the kitchen window. Now it seemed May had
left her children to fend for themselves, and so I fed them. I
watched the kittens eat for a while, then came back in and
began to write. I put in a solid few hours before Kip returned, and we made plans for a drive into Morelia, the city
a half hour away. Kip had a meeting with another veterinarian, and I would sightsee and shop. Later, Kip would meet
me in the cathedral for an organ recital.

Kip dropped me off in the square and I bought some
sweet custardlike bars with coconut on top and figs embed-
ded in them, then went into the cathedral. It was dark in
there, cool and still. Christ looked pained on his cross while
the Virgin looked compassionate and kind on top of her
world. I sat in a pew, took a deep breath of air spiced with incense. In the silent stillness, all my feelings of loss and joy
and fear ran up and down and through me. It was as though
kind ears were listening and waiting; the very air was quiet
with compassion, and it felt safe to spill feelings that had
been a secret even to me. I bent my head into my hands and
felt, simply, lost—as I remembered another dream I'd had
the night before. In that dream I had a pain, pushed once,
and gave birth to a beautiful baby girl. I experienced such a
feeling of contentment and well-being that I thought, So
this is how an infant feels when she drinks from her mother's

breast. Then, still in the dream, with a jolt, I realized I wouldn't be able to have a career, and that the father was Nigel. Suddenly, I felt like an orphan.

Awake, it made no sense. I was confusing motherhood with being a baby. I'd felt contentment like a baby drinking from a breast, but I was the mother, the one drunk from. Or was it possible that being a mother could give you such contentment? I'd never experienced that. But in the dream, I'd ended up feeling like an orphan, who'd been wanted for a brief moment but wasn't wanted anymore. Was I the rejecter or the rejected—or were they the same thing? Was this dream about a child homesick for her mother or about a mother rejecting her child?

All I knew was I felt as bad as I'd ever felt in my life, and I started to cry.

In the back of the church, an organ struck the first chords of some Mozart. The music was so powerfully moving that it shook me out of myself. I wiped my eyes with the bottom of my shirt and looked around. An open dark-mahogany confessional stood at the back of the church, in which a handsome priest with salt-and-pepper hair sat with his chin in his hand and his head bowed, listening. He was lit from above, like a painting. Next to him, talking into his ear, was an elegantly dressed woman with her dog, a little terrier, staring longingly up at her. I couldn't tell if it was the dog's devotion or the woman's faith or the priest's compassion, or all of these things, but the vision of them filled me with so much longing, I doubled over weeping, remembering now the kittens in the dream I'd had that morning. They were, of course, the kittens in my backyard, and they were also the kittens that a stray cat had had in my kitchen one freezing-cold winter evening back in Connecticut, the winter after my husband, Ray, had left. There were six kittens in that kitchen. I didn't know what to do with them, swarming underfoot, overwhelming me with a feeling of being out of control. Did the need of the helpless make me feel out of control? Could I ever love if this was true? A brick hit me in my chest. I found myself remembering that baby I'd aborted, the one I'd had with Nigel. I'd never thought much about the abortion, not even as I lay in the recovery room, awaking from the anesthesia, hearing the moans of the woman next to me, "My baby, my baby." I did not cry. I refused to be sad. I would not have regret. I was controlling my own body; I was doing the only thing I could at the time. But inside, I must have suffered at the loss, and had never confronted my true feelings. Until I entered that church. Weeping, I calculated my baby's age, eight, thought she'd been a girl like the baby in the dream, and wept, mourning for the first time the loss of her.

When I came up for air, I found myself staring at the painting of the Virgin of Guadalupe on the side wall. There was sadness in her face, and love. After Kip and I drove home that night, I dug her out of the closet and hung her on our dining-room wall above the yellow roses.

I mourned the baby I'd killed back then, I've mourned my baby since, and I don't want to mourn anymore, especially not as a result of Father Jozo's finger-pointing sermonizing.

Back in bed that afternoon, trying to keep warm, I'm exhausted from all the crying and churchgoing, the "salty tears in bleeding flesh," the lectern pounding, all this regret. I do not want to be a crazy, sign-seeing, rose-smelling, rigid, right-to-life Catholic. I do not want to participate in this pilgrimage anymore. I've had enough. I will attend Father's Slavko's lecture this afternoon, but I won't attend mass at Saint James. I will go for a beer.

After the lecture, I pull on my black coat, wrap a scarf around my neck, yank my beret over my ears, and head for the door. But the moment I reach the door, Father Slavko, who has hung back uncharacteristically, reaches the door, too. "Going to church?" he asks.

"No. I don't know." Suddenly I don't.

"I'll give you a ride."

In the car I say, "I'm a journalist. I don't believe."

He looks at me and smiles, but not kindly exactly, more like he's waiting for the punch line to a joke.

"I'd like to interview you," I say.

"What for?"

"To hear about miracles, cures—to get the history straight."

"These are not important things. You come in the side door with me. Get a good seat."

I sit three rows from the front and wait. This night in church is different. It's the first time Father Slavko will lead the service. Someone has hung a screen up high to the left of the altar, on which the phonetic pronunciations for the

Serbo-Croatian words to the hymns are projected. Father Slavko plays the piano and a group of kids plays guitars and sings around him as the rest of us, numbering thousands, sing too. Then, when the little concert is done, the screen remains for the hymns we sing after every ten Hail Marys, but Father Slavko has left the piano.

He is kneeling at the altar, his forehead bent to the ground for an hour and a half, the microphone at his lips, leading the rosary in a voice that comes from someplace I know I have never been.

I wonder if it's a place I could ever get to—if I had the courage, if I had the faith.

❦

Mary gives monthly "messages for the world" from Medjugorje. In one of her messages this is what she said: "If they can't believe in God, they should spend at least five minutes a day in silent meditation. During that time they should think about the God they say doesn't exist."

Mary shows herself the way people would like to see her. In Africa she is black. In Mexico she has dark skin. Our Lady speaks all languages, is indescribably beautiful, and dresses in amazing costumes, which she changes for special occasions—on holidays she favors gold. Wherever she is, she announces her presence by perfuming the air with roses. Her apparitions are like visits, at which she comes for a period of time, tells you things you need to hear, then listens. And like any visiting mother she

worries about you and tells you what you need to do to feel bet-
ter. Basically, she tells you to pray, and not just for yourself but
for one another. She asks you to pray for the whole world.

She weeps when she sees us fighting or going to war. Tears fall
during her visits; they fall from her face frozen in a statue, they
fall from her face painted on canvas, masonite, and wood. Vio-
lence makes her cry blood sometimes. Violence killed her son.
"Love one another," Mary says. "Pray to heal the world."

CHAPTER TEN

*B*efore confession, I sit outside Father Freed's door and shiver through bouts of anxiety as I wait. Terrified of revealing my heart, I begin to resist. Am I buying all this religious stuff lock, stock, and flaming heart? People on this retreat even believe in the literal location of a heaven and hell. They believe your guardian angel leads you to the only empty parking place in a parking lot. And they believe the closer you get to God, the more hotly the devil pursues you. Father Slavko says that Satan's biggest triumph is getting people to believe he doesn't exist.

I try to remember when it was, exactly, that I switched to the devil's camp and lost God, and decide there was no single moment, that it happened more like a shifting of the San Andreas fault. I remember that in the summer after the sixth grade, the same summer I got my period, I busted into the new junior high school under construction, shouting the song from *Popeye*, "Da da dadada da dada. . . ." I broke windows, slit open bags of cement, tossed the powder in the air, and tap-danced in it. I threw nails everywhere. I didn't know why I was doing this. But I did know that I was being bad, and it was fun. When I saw the story in the paper, how "vandals" had broken into the school, and that "juvenile delinquents" were suspected, it was official.

By high school, I was standing in front of the mirror, entertaining myself with the ugly faces I could make and fantasizing that the devil was looking out through my eyes. I daydreamed that I was a devil sitting on girls' shoulders, tempting them to tell that lie, spread that gossip, steal those earrings, fuck that boy.

When I got pregnant, I believed I'd received God's punishment and that he'd betrayed and abandoned me, even though I hadn't really believed in him since I'd learned about evolution in the seventh grade, and I hadn't really believed in the devil, either. Or did I believe? Because whenever the world got scary, I still cried, "Please, dear God. . . ." But after I got pregnant at seventeen, I denounced God, the devil, religion, forever. All of it. Lock, stock, and flaming heart.

And here I am, three decades later, about to confess everything and beg forgiveness.

A mountain of toilet paper rolls is piled in a corner of the storage room where I sit across from Father Freed on a folding chair to make my confession. The room smells like a sewer, because sewage has backed up into the bathroom next door.

"Forgive me, Father, for I have sinned," I say. "It has been thirty-five years since my last confession." I giggle. Father Freed smiles kindly and waits. I burst into tears. "I feel like

I'm going crazy. All these people talking about suffering. Talking about Christ's salty blood dripping into his wounds. It's sick. They get off on it. They think suffering is good. Suffering is part of life, but they look for it, indulge in it to be more holy or something . . . it's sick. I never asked Christ to die for my sins. I never asked him to be crucified. I don't even like him. He's a whiner. He says, 'Look at me. I suffered for your sins. You should be grateful, but what do you do? Sin, sin, sin.' I feel love for Mary. I really do. But this Christ martyr and his damned suffering—I'm sick of it. I spent my whole life trying not to feel guilty. I'm crippled with guilt. Why would I want to be a Catholic and make it worse? I shouldn't even be here. I can't stand this. I'm going crazy. I feel awful."

"Christ does not want you to suffer."

"But these people . . ."

"This group is particularly zealous."

"Not all Catholics are like that?"

"No." He smiles.

"You're not? You don't think you should wear a hair shirt or climb the mountain barefoot or be grateful that the sewage backed up into your bathroom so you can offer it up to God?"

"No. As a matter of fact, there *is* sewage backing up into my room, and I've requested a transfer."

"Really?" I laugh.

"Honest to God. Now, is there anything troubling you?"

"I had an abortion. I had to. I can't even say I wouldn't do it again, and I'd never take away another woman's right to choose. Maybe if I'd had faith, like Mary, I wouldn't have had that abortion. I might have believed everything would work out for the better. But I didn't have faith. And I still can't imagine my life if I'd had that child. I was wild. I had sex indiscriminately for many years. I didn't even enjoy it. It was the times. I was making a political point. Probably I was looking for love and couldn't even admit it. I have gossiped cruelly. I have hated. I am critical and judgmental. I don't like people I don't even know. It makes me feel shitty. I don't want to do it. I really do want to look with the eyes of love. To love as God loves, like Father Slavko says. But I'm mean. I make fun. That's what I do. That's who I am. I've always been like that. Or at least since I was twelve. That's really when I stopped believing in God. Do you think I'm possessed by the devil?"

"I do not."

"How do you know?"

"You are not as bad as you think."

"I'm selfish. I have said no to love. I was the worst mother. I never once put my son's needs before mine. I lived with three different men. Disasters. I always did what I needed to do for me, never what was best for my son. I always felt guilty, which made me depressed, which made me resentful. I used to say, 'I'm like an older sister, and you're like my younger brother.' I'm like one of those cats who abandons her litter. I never wanted to be a mother. Not even when I was a kid. I hated baby dolls. I had postnatal depression till my son left for college. And my son suffers for it. He feels like he wasn't loved. I damaged him. He's depressed and he's angry."

"Do you speak of these things?"

"Kind of. A little."

"Have you asked for his forgiveness?"

"I'm not sure."

"It would be good if you could encourage him to speak, to acknowledge his pain."

"Yes."

"I would like you to pray to the Blessed Mother for help. Ask her to help you be close to your son, to help you to mother."

"I do all the time. I think that's why I'm so attracted to her. Because I want to learn to be a mother. That and because I want a mother for myself. I want to learn how to trust, to stop taking every step expecting a pitfall."

"I'd also like you to pray to the Virgin of Guadalupe. Do you know who she is?"

"Of course. I lived in Mexico."

"I have a special devotion to Guadalupe. My church is called the Virgin of Guadalupe. She's the saint of the unborn. She has two tassels on her dress. That's the symbol for the unborn. Pray to her to help you heal from your abortion. You need to forgive yourself. God forgives you. He loves you exactly the way you are . . . not the way you think you should be."

"Thank you, Father."

"I would also like you to go to the chapel and sit with Jesus."

"I have adoration tonight. For an hour." I nearly shouted in my panic. "I haven't done it yet."

"Good. I want you to go to adoration and not pray prayers. I want you to just sit there and tell Jesus exactly what you told me. Confess everything and tell him exactly how you feel about him. Then just sit, and listen."

The adoration room looks like a room in a community center that's been donated to shelter people during a flood. There are twenty people on their knees praying, lying in their sleeping bags in corners, or sitting cross-legged with blankets wrapped around them, staring at the monstrance containing the body of Christ. This has been going on the whole time, and I'd no idea.

Since I began doing Mary research, I've read many times that Mary is the intermediary between her son and us. She brings us to her son. That is her role and her job. She is the conduit between the human and the divine. She was human herself but gave birth to God. It is through her that Jesus has his humanity. And by continually giving birth to faith, she continues to give birth to her son.

I promised Father Freed to talk to Jesus, and I want to do it for Mary. He is her son, and she would like this. So I sit there and I repeat in my mind what I said to Father Freed, which takes much less than an hour. So while I'm sitting there, I ask Mary to help me understand why I should love her son and to help me give up my prejudices against him for being a man, and all that manhood conveys: judge and ruler, oppressor of women, testosterone driven, boss and superior.

I close my eyes and picture Mary taking both my hands and pulling me to stand. She leads me to her son, who takes my hand, and I stand between them, one hand in Mary's and one hand in Jesus'.

I do not think this is a true adoration. But it is a beginning.

In bed that night I think how wonderful and light I will feel if I can really feel forgiven.

And then I wonder whom I can forgive.

Ray. My husband. I'd never even learned to call him my ex-husband, and now he's dead. Four months before I came to Medjugorje, Jason called me in California. He'd received a phone call from Ray's second ex-wife, Donna. Ray had died at forty-seven of AIDS-related symptoms. Jason and I were invited to the funeral.

Jason had seen his father only once after Ray left when Jason was thirteen months old. Jason was eleven, and we were living with Nigel, when he suddenly became interested in his father. "Where is he? Could we find him?" he asked one afternoon. And so I tracked Ray down through his mother. Ray was living two hours away, in Greenwood Lake, and he invited Jason to come visit.

Jason woke me up before dawn, and as we ate English muffins, watching the sunrise through our windows, I asked, "Are you scared?"

"How will I know what he looks like?"

There'd never been a picture of his father in Jason's, or in any, room. My box of pictures was stored in my parents' attic. "Don't worry, Jase." I patted his hand across the table. "He'll recognize you."

Jason withdrew his hand, put down his English muffin, and stared at the middle of the table.

"You'll be the only kid stepping off the bus alone. He'll come to you. Just stand there. . . . He has black hair. He's not tall, and he's not short—he's medium. I'm giving you money. If he doesn't come, call me up. I'll wait at home. I'll come and get you."

"Does he look like me?"

"A little. Not much." There was a downward slant of the eye, a slouchiness in the shoulders, an occasional slant of the head or way of careening around in the middle of a step. These similarities were subtle and over the years had been easy to ignore.

At Port Authority, Jason put his backpack on, took the ticket from me, and climbed the stairs of the bus. He was so small; the backpack so huge. It was dark in the station, and the windows in the bus were tinted, so I couldn't see which seat he took or if he was waving. I waved to them all.

Climbing back down the bus steps on Sunday, Jason seemed shy. He was carrying a Baggie of homemade chocolate-chip cookies. We kissed hello. "What's this?" I said, pointing to the cookies.

"He lives with a woman named Linda. She baked them for me."

"Did you like her?"

"Um-hmm." He nodded. "She has a daughter named Juice."

"Juice?"

"Because she likes it. She was only a baby. She couldn't talk yet."

"And your father?"

"He was nice. His teeth were bad."

"What did you do?"

"We went to the bar. He gave me quarters for pinball. Sunday we went to see *Rocky II*."

"Did you like your father?"

"Yeah. He gave me twenty dollars."

"What are you going to do with it?"

"Save it, maybe."

"You going to see him again?"

"Yeah. I want to."

Jason never heard from his father again.

The next year, we were living on Avenue A when Jase had his twelfth birthday. Juano and Amaal came and we had an ice cream cake; then afterwards Jason brushed his teeth at the kitchen sink, our only sink, before bed. After he wiped his mouth with a towel he said, not looking at me, "How will we know if my father's dead? We should find out. We could get social security."

"What would you prefer, Jase? Social security or a birthday card?" I asked.

"A birthday card."

I hugged him.

Then, seventeen years later, we heard Ray was dead.

Ray's ex-wife had our New York number because I'd spoken to her when Jason graduated from high school and I'd called Greenwood Lake information to invite Ray to the ceremony. Donna and Ray had separated when Jason had visited his father. They were now divorced but she had Ray's phone number and gave it to me. Before I hung up, we had a nice chat.

Donna told me she was going to community college to become a nurse, and that her two daughters were real good, smart girls. Donna had been seventeen when she'd become pregnant by Ray, just like I'd been. Her oldest daughter, Jessie, had been nearly the same age as Jason, a year and a half, and Donna had been pregnant with her second child, Jenny, when Ray deserted. "I had pork chops on the stove and he never came home."

A few weeks later, she found out Ray had shacked up with her best friend. "She's a dog. Who could do that, then face me in the supermarket? She should leave town. I'll be damned if I will."

I told her how I wanted Ray to know that his son had been a straight-A student at Stuyvesant High School, and that he'd won a scholarship to a very good college. I wanted Ray to feel proud, and I wanted Jason to have a father at his graduation.

"Believe me, Bev," Ray had said when I called, "he don't want to know his old man. I got bleeding ulcers, pancreatitis. I'm in and out of the VA hospital. When I get my shit together . . ."

I did not tell Jason I'd reached his father and he'd refused to come to his graduation. I had told him, though, that he had two sisters, and Jason had said that maybe once he got his driver's license he'd take a ride up there to meet them; but he never did. The time had come for us to meet Donna and her two daughters.

I'd flown to New York to accompany Jason to the funeral in Greenwood Lake. Jason had a therapist's appointment in the morning, then picked me up in his VW Rabbit. As we drove through a stretch of bumper-to-bumper traffic on Thirty-third Street, Jason said, "We have to talk."

My son had never said those words to me in his life.

"I'm really angry with you." He'd never said those words, either. My stomach tightened, even though this is what I'd been praying for. "I'm really angry with you for not saying right away that you'd come with me to the funeral."

I'd had a conflict, a reporting assignment for the radio documentary, and it had taken me till the next morning to say yes. Jason was absolutely right. If I'd had a scheduled interview with God himself, I still shouldn't have even blinked at agreeing to escort my son.

"I never ask for things, because I'm afraid you'll say no," he said. "It's easier not to ask than to face being disappointed. You're a selfish person."

It was true. My own needs had always been more important than my son's. This was not the way love acts; this is not what a child deserves. It had taken such courage, I knew, for him to speak. I closed my eyes in the car and asked Mary to show me how to help, to grant me the grace to change and to give to my son in ways I didn't even know how. I wish I had said, "I'm sorry. I love you. I wish I could do it over again, because I know how I've hurt you." But I didn't. I said, "It must have been horrible to have a mother who never put you first. Mothers are supposed to do that."

His eyes filled with tears.

In Greenwood Lake we had to stop our car to make way for a jiggly woman in a muumuu crossing the road. Her hair was dirty-blond, long and stringy. Despite the early-spring chill, she wasn't wearing a sweater. Her belly hung halfway to her knees, and you just knew she had missing teeth. Jase and I looked at each other and said nothing, although we both knew what the other was thinking: Please don't let that be Ray's ex-wife. We wanted her and her daughters to be great. I wanted Jase to have sisters whose genes he'd be proud to share.

The restaurant was constructed of logs and had fake tulips stuck into the ground along the sidewalk. When I pointed them out to Jason, he laughed, which might have been the first time he'd loosened up since I'd come east.

We entered a wood-paneled bar, beyond which was the dining room with big windows facing the lake. The moment we stepped in the door, three attractive women arose from a table in the dining room, smiling. Donna was nothing like the woman we'd seen on the road. She was slender and lively and had a lovely smile. "Well . . ." We looked at each other.

"Wow," I said.

"This is my youngest." She pulled on Jenny's arm. Jenny looked at me, then at Jason, and giggled. Her large green eyes slanted downward like her father's—like Jason's—only more so. I'd been told by her mother that, at eighteen, she'd just had a baby six months ago. It had been her idea to look up her father, and they'd found him, one hundred pounds, stricken with AIDS, and dying in a hospital a few towns away.

Jenny's older sister, Jessie, seemed relieved to release her hand from my handshake. She looked away as soon as our eyes met. Her coloring, her nose, her cheekbones, her chin were exactly Jason's. But she seemed to be trying to tamp down her beauty. Her hair was pulled severely into a bun, but you could see hundreds of little kinks that gave away its lush curliness.

They'd reserved a table at the far end at a window overlooking the lake. Jenny's fiancé, a short, handsome young man, took off his baseball cap and joined us. They looked like high-school kids and were still living in Donna's house. Jessie had a job in a bank but still lived at home too.

Jase and I, in our expensive haircuts and fashionable city clothes, polished by our elite educations, could hardly speak to each other. We'd left the working class while Donna and her daughters hadn't. But they were close and warm with one another, a family. How much had I sacrificed for my ambition?

We all ordered drinks, then food. And we talked.

Jessie had not wanted to visit her father in the hospital, but Jenny and her mother had visited Ray every three weeks for the last six months of his life. Jenny had brought her baby to meet him. By the time he died, Ray was incoherent. He'd had a girlfriend, who had taken his few possessions from the hospital, including a crocheted comforter that Jenny wanted. She was planning on tracking the girlfriend down. They were all wondering if the woman would show up at the funeral tomorrow.

"I doubt it." Donna sounded a little jealous.

"I'm pissed at him." Jessie broke her silence. "When I was around seven my mother was going out with a friend of my father's. My father traveled all the way across the state to stand in the street and scream up at the window, 'That's my woman, that's my woman.' And there I was, his own daughter, right under his nose. And he didn't even look."

I looked at Donna, and she looked at me and shrugged.

Jason told us the story about hunting his father down and that he used to want to find out if his father was dead because then he could get social security.

"Jessie used to say the same thing," Donna said. Brother and sister looked at each other and smiled. "There was this girl," Jenny said. "It was probably Juice. She used to go around school saying that Ray wasn't her father but he loved her more than me. So one day I just had to beat her up." She sat taller in her chair and grinned.

Donna wanted to go to the bar for a smoke, and Jenny and I went with her. "One thing," I said, "you have to hand it to Ray: he chose great women and he had great kids. It's amazing he got you pregnant at seventeen, too."

"Oh, no. I can't blame him for that. He didn't want to. He said I was too young. I was a virgin and there was a lot of pressure to have sex. I seduced him. I convinced him. I refuse to be mad at him. It doesn't do me any good, and he was incapable. He was."

He was incapable of not lying; he was incapable of being good to himself or to anyone else. It was true.

When we returned to the table, Jessie and Jason seemed to

be enjoying themselves. Donna said, "One time Ray called out of the blue. I hadn't heard from him for a couple of years. He needed a hundred dollars to get to Florida. He's a caddie and it was winter. He swore somebody owed him money and as soon as he got it he'd pay me back. You know how that goes. So I says, 'I don't know, Ray. That's one hundred dollars less of a Christmas your daughters are going to have. I'll have to ask them.' I asked them and they told me to do whatever I wanted. 'It's up to you, Mom,' they said. But he never called back. And I'd be damned if I was going to hunt him down."

How does a person get to be like Donna? Generous, kind, warmhearted, forgiving. Keeping that man in her life when he'd done her so wrong. Had she been a girlfriend of mine, I would have told her to get her head examined. I would have said, "You don't owe him anything—he got himself in the jam, he can get himself out." I'd have said, "Think of your kids and their Christmas, not that no-good waste-of-a-human-life junkie ex-husband. I don't know how you can even speak to him." But maybe then her kids wouldn't have learned kindness, compassion, selflessness. Maybe they would have felt good sacrificing for their father, even a father who'd left them in the cold. I didn't know. I didn't know anything, except that somehow Ray had found a good woman, who'd loved him till he died.

The next morning Jason and I were the first to arrive at the church and sat silently in a pew toward the front. When Jason's sisters arrived, they told him to move over and sat next to him. I could feel Jason kind of melt beside me. I imagined him the older brother. His sisters would tease, maybe fuss over him. Tell him what to wear, to grow his hair longer, let it go curly. They'd tease him about his J. Crew catalog taste in girlfriends. He'd hassle them about their guys. Finally, Jason would have a family.

Donna sat behind us between two of her relatives. She patted her girls', then Jason's, shoulders. Donna and I held hands for a second.

Besides us, Ray's widowed sister-in-law, her son, and a few people from Donna's family were all who attended Ray's funeral. Ray's mother was still alive, and living in a nursing home in Connecticut, but she didn't come.

The priest looked drunk as he wove to the top of the aisle for his eulogy. He tucked his hands inside his vestments and said grimly, "Animals were put on the earth to serve humans. Humans were put on earth to serve God. And believe me, I know about sneaking a bottle of scotch into the veterans' ward, and I'm not talking about when I was a priest. God rest Ray Budrow's soul. He is at peace." He nodded and turned back to prepare the host. The mass took all of twenty minutes.

On our drive back to the city, I asked Jason how he felt.

"I don't feel anything," he said abruptly.

Alone with me again, my son was a million miles away, buried in an avalanche of ice. I was in agony; I did not know how to melt his anger.

The next morning, back home in LA, it was a Sunday and spring and the wisteria was in bloom. I felt light and filled with energy and stepped out into the sun first thing. I went to a service at a New Agey church I'd been to before. The five hundred people at the service smiled in that California-dreamy sunshine way. The minister was black and charismatic, and the rock-and-roll gospel music sublime. The minister told of a boy whose fingers grew back through prayer. He said God was in us and through us and with us. We should not pray through a sense of lack but in the knowledge that everything we want is already there, inside us, where God lives. He said we were God's instruments of love in the world. We all stood and sang a song that began, "I surrender, I surrender, I surrender. . . ." It felt so good. As soon as I got home I planted a cherry tomato plant and a basil plant in pots, then set them in the sun on the terrace. I baked chocolate-chip cookies and called some friends. Only after they'd left and the sun began to set and I was walking on the beach, saying a rosary, which I had managed to do almost every day for maybe a month, did I remember that this day was my anniversary. That twenty-eight years ago I married Ray Budrow. I also remembered that I had been depressed on every April 27 for twenty-eight years.

And now here I am, in bed in Medjugorje, remembering and crying at the same time. I do not cry for the man Ray might have been or the man he had been. I don't cry for my son, who never knew his father, or for the stone-cold anger in my son's heart. I don't cry for the coming together of two people, for the bed we shared, for Ray so young and all dusty and tired from work, for the laughing we couldn't stop, high on marijuana, for the breeze through a van with an American flag painted on its side, and Ray and I clutching each other in the back of it high on horse tranquilizers, the world slow as syrup and our son at home asleep in his crib, us holding on tight, dizzy and high, the music on the radio a trigger to yell at the top of our lungs, "Holy Christ!" holding on for dear life. I don't cry for Ray's life, so pain filled, so short. I don't cry for him. I don't cry for me, or his son, or his other wife, or his daughters. Instead, I say a rosary, and the images of those two girls and my son at dinner come to me. There was something the same in the three of them, something sweet and warm, something good and kind, and it was in their father, too. Ray, at his core, was a sweet and dear person. Ray was damaged, and he'd suffered more than anyone he ever hurt. I feel a deep well of sorrow for him, which I knew to be the beginning of forgiveness. It had taken twenty-five years.

I open the Bible to Corinthians: "Love is patient; love is kind; love is not envious or boastful or arrogant or rude. . . . It bears all things, believes all things, hopes all things, endures all things. . . ."

I so want to try.

Then, next morning, at my first communion in thirty-five years, after the host has been turned into the body of Christ, I kneel and say the same words I've said at masses twice every day in Medjugorje: "Lord, I am not worthy to receive you, but only say the word and I shall be healed."

Only, this time I really hear them. This time when Father

Freed walks from person to person offering communion, I do not bow my head to refuse it but raise my face to him. As the host melts on my tongue, I imagine forgiveness like a warm stream, flowing to my heart and bathing it with love, healing it. My tears fall, and fall, like rose petals from heaven.

❧

Mary is a woman who gets what she wants.

When Mary appeared in 1858 to Bernadette Soubirous at Lourdes, one of the world's most renowned apparition sites, the Church and Mary herself were under siege by French atheists and rationalists. The doctrine of the Immaculate Conception, which had just been made dogma a few years earlier, was being ridiculed.

Fourteen-year-old Bernadette was not a very bright child; perhaps that's why Mary chose her. Bernadette said that when she asked the beautiful Lady who she was, as the bishop had instructed her to do, the Lady said, "I am the Immaculate Conception," words Bernadette had been afraid she'd forget, and so had repeated them over and over until she returned to the bishop. No one who knew Bernadette could believe that she had come up with the words on her own.

Almost three decades before she appeared to Bernadette, Mary had appeared in Paris to a young nun named Catherine Labouré. Mary gave Catherine a vision of a medal Mary wanted minted, on which she called herself the Immaculate Conception. After hundreds of healings were reported by people wearing the medal, it was declared miraculous, which put some heat on the powers that be to make Mary's Immaculate Conception dogma. (The Immaculate Conception does not refer to Jesus' being conceived without the act of sex, but to Mary's having been born without the stain of Original Sin, making her a perfect vessel to receive the Lord.)

The dogma of the Immaculate Conception was instituted in 1854, but four years later it was still under fire, so Mary appeared again, this time to Bernadette, to bring attention to and to defend her doctrine.

The clergy and the town government were skeptical, and some were downright hostile, but the people followed Bernadette in droves to the dump where Mary appeared. When a large crowd had gathered, Our Lady asked Bernadette to dig in the dirt, which released the underground spring that became the famous healing waters of Lourdes.

Bernadette went to live in a convent in nearby Nevers, where she was not embraced by her fellow sisters, who were jealous of all the attention she had received. During outings, Bernadette would be seen walking all alone, yards behind the other nuns. Our Lady had told Bernadette, "I do not promise you happiness in this life, but in the next."

Bernadette died at thirty-five, and some years later her body was exhumed and found to be incorrupt. I believe she also smells of roses. Bernadette was canonized as a saint and in a glass coffin in the little church in Nevers, her body is exhibited, as fresh as the day she died.

CHAPTER ELEVEN

*I*t's our last morning of fasting, after which we move back to the private houses and are set free for lunch. Later in the afternoon we will pile onto a bus and hike up Mount Krizevac.

We've been told that the Virgin Mary will appear to Mirjana the next day on a hill, and that when Mary appears, she automatically blesses everything you bring to her. I shop like I've won a raffle and the prize is to be let loose in a store for an hour. I buy a hundred Medjugorje medals with Mary on one side and Saint James Church on the other. I buy refrigerator magnets of the Virgin, and Saint Benedict medals I'm told will drive away evil and cure animals of illness. I buy a thin, delicate-looking Virgin and also a crucifix made of white pressed marble, which I plan to hang on a white wall. And I stock up on rosaries: I buy a hundred plastic Day-Glo rosaries, a dozen made of small gold beads connected by a thin strand of silver, and six made of crushed rose petals. I am planning to bring them all to the apparition tomorrow; and then back home when I hand them out as souvenirs and good-luck charms, I will say that they've been blessed by the Mother of God, and let everyone make of it what they like.

I have become converted to the use of the rosary as a weapon against evil, a magic ring of words that helps you to meditate on peace and to feel it—a magnet that draws Mary into your heart. My friends and acquaintances will all have a rosary in their houses, and if they ever feel the desire or need to pray on one, they'll be prepared.

The sisters and I order a mixed plate of meats, a big green salad with tomatoes, and each drink a beer for lunch before we board our bus, which winds up roads that sometimes seem so narrow I fear we'll fall off their edge. At the base of Mount Krizevac there are a couple of empty cafes, but fifty yards up the trail we are in the wilderness. It's a steep climb that will take over two hours. At intervals are the fourteen stations of the cross—depictions of Christ's Passion, beginning with his Agony in the Garden and ending at the top of the mountain with his Resurrection. Also at the top is the cement cross the villagers built at the turn of the century to consecrate their village to Mary. I've been told that you can leave something you don't want at the foot of the cross. I haven't decided yet what that will be, but I'm hoping something will occur to me on the hike up.

I feel like I've been let loose from a confinement. My legs want to do a jig as I climb up the steep trail, feeling my body come awake. Deprivation really does have its rewards: mainly how appreciative you feel when it's over. I long to walk at a clip and work up a sweat, which I do, but then am stuck waiting for my fellow pilgrims to catch up at each station. James, a nineteen-year-old with shoulder-length hair and black polish on his toenails, takes a long time because he's walking barefoot. Somehow, I don't think the gesture strange; I think it's youthful and passionate, and wonder at how my perspective on things is beginning to change.

We have to wait even longer for Mrs. Benedetti, who has had a stroke and is taking baby steps with two canes. At the second station, she collapses on a rock and starts to cry. "I wanted to climb to the top for Our Lady. I promised her, but I can't." One of the nurses, who works at a hospice for the terminally ill, a woman who has come to Medjugorje for discernment (to find out if she has a calling to become a nun), offers to stay behind with Mrs. Benedetti, and so we leave them behind.

The cross at the top is huge and made of concrete. I sit on the platform at its base and drink in the view of the little village nestled amid the vineyards and forests, and as I see a trail of dark smoke curl from a chimney, I know what I will leave at the cross: my pride—my bugaboo, the thorn in my side. It has made me lie about what I really want and hide who I really am, even to myself. Pride has made me so concerned with image, I forget my heart.

I know what my heart wants: Mary in my life, to pray rosaries, light candles, kneel in churches, talk to the Mother of God every day. People will call me a weirdo, a born-again Christian, and this will hurt my pride. So I leave it at the foot of the cross and head back down the mountain.

At the bottom, I see Mrs. Benedetti sitting on a veranda, beaming. "What happened to you?" I ask.

She holds up the silver, half-dollar-sized Mary medal that has hung around her neck every day. "I made it to the fourth station, and look. . . ."

Mary's silver face has turned gold.

I hold the medal, still dangling on its chain, in my hand, and then I kiss Mrs. Benedetti, who says, "God bless."

"God bless *you*," I say.

The next morning is Saturday, and Mirjana's apparition is scheduled to begin at noon. It's our last full day in Medjugorje before we leave for Italy the next morning, so I rummage through the stores looking for the perfect Mary statue, and I find it. She's wearing a creamy white dress covered by a deep blue cape through which you can see the outline of her knee under its folds. Her hair is dark brown and her expression peaceful and lovely as she points to the red heart flaming on her chest. She is a foot tall and made of marble and absolutely perfect except for the fact that she's as heavy as a sack of potatoes. I worry about lugging her around in my baggage but know I'll be grateful to have her once I reach home. In the same store are a few six-inch-high, slightly less detailed duplicates of the same statue; I buy three of these, too.

After I buy them I hurry back to my room and heap them along with all the rosaries and medals and magnets into two shopping bags. At the last moment, I remember my other statue, the one with the tear on Mary's cheek that Beatrice had given me. I grab a third shopping bag and drop it in there, then stop by the sisters' room to pick them up, but Alma declines to come, because she's sick with the flu. We wish her a speedy recovery, then Arlene takes her bag of holy souvenirs and we walk together through a vineyard down a lane by some houses to a field, where thousands have already gathered. We climb a hill and find a good spot on a stone wall, from which we can see Mirjana a hundred yards away. A group of Filipinos crowds around us as the minutes pass, and I balance myself precariously until Arlene graciously relieves me of one of my bags.

The rosary begins, and the voices echoing off the surrounding hills sound like a choir. The temperature is deliciously warm, the sky shockingly blue in its brilliance, the air portentously still and peaceful. As we pray on our rosaries, Arlene nods toward the cross on Mount Krizevac, which seems to be pulsating and glowing gold. It could be a trick of the sun, so I don't believe I am seeing one of the miracles I've heard about. Then I see, down on the road far below, a nun taking remarkably long strides, walking at a determined clip. She's all in gray and wearing a long skirt and a veil that falls just below her waist and flares behind like wings.

There's something about her. She doesn't look like any nun I've ever seen; her presence is too big. She reminds me of the statue Beatrice gave me; then I remember that Mirjana said that Our Lady wears gray in Medjugorje, and think: Oh, my God, it's Mary. She rounds a bend and goes out of sight, so I do not point her out to Arlene—and besides, I'm afraid my imagination is getting carried away. But I can't help thinking that if that's Mary, she's one lady on a mission.

Some minutes later, everyone falls silent, as is the custom, because Mirjana is having her vision.

There's the sense of a collectively held breath. I close my eyes and try to feel Our Lady's presence, and what I feel is hard to describe. It's like the feeling you get when you've spent the entire day outdoors, in nature. After hours of being in the sun and in the open air with no roof over your head, you possess a certain euphoria, an expansiveness under the skin, a feeling like you're floating. And that's what I feel that noontime after being outside for only an hour.

The apparition ends and Mirjana appears to be weeping, supported by two men. We recite the concluding rosary-and-a-half with the crowd; then Arlene and I walk down to a little cafe at the bottom of the hill to have cappuccinos. We order; then Arlene looks in the bag she's been holding for me and says, "Your statue fell out of its box. Oh, no—it's broken."

I take the bag and lift out the statue Beatrice had given me. Mary's outstretched hand has broken off. I find the hand at the bottom of the bag, then hold the little hand in mine for a moment before I position it back at the end of the statue's arm. I'm disappointed it's broken but relieved to know I can glue it back.

I take the box out to replace the statue and see that it isn't open and do not understand how the statue could have fallen out. I hold the statue up and look at it. The tear and its shiny track have disappeared from Mary's face.

My heart feels it's between a giggle and a tear.

Arlene and I stare at each other, then turn the bag inside

out. There is no chip of a tear and no roughness on the statue's cheek.

Mirjana's words come to mind: "Every prayer you say for a nonbeliever takes a tear from Our Mother's face." I'd gone to confession and received communion after thirty-five years, and Mary has stopped crying.

Walking back to our house, we run into Father Freed and I excitedly tell him what happened as I pull the statue out of the bag and hand it to him. Father Freed runs his thumb over the statue's cheek, and it comes to me: "Do you think her hand broke off because she wants to give me a hand?" I ask him.

Father Freed hesitates.

"You think it means I'm supposed to give *her* a hand?"

"I think it means both," Father Freed says as the sun shoots a beam like a spotlight through the middle of a cloud straight to the tops of our heads. "Oh, my God," we all say, and my insides vibrate like a tuning fork.

On our way back to our house, I feel Mary all around, and so near, like a steady hand at the small of my back, a kiss on the top of my head, a cape of comfort wrapping me in. Arlene and I pass through a field that was green just that morning but is now carpeted with white moon-faced flowers turned toward the sky. I breathe deeply, not surprised by anything anymore, but so grateful, and tranquil. I'm drugged with love.

Then, when we reach our house, a half-dozen women call down to us from the balcony. "Look at the sun."

It's spinning.

I know that I'm lucky, and blessed. I'm being given signs to help me believe, to strengthen my faith. I know that when I tell other people about this, they won't believe it happened. I'm seeing it, and it's hard for me to believe, too. I am staring directly at the sun, which is physiologically impossible to do, as light rays spin in a pinwheel and bloom sunset colors in every direction into the sky.

We continue to watch from the balcony, singing hymns for the next two hours as it sets. When a man walks by, we yell down, "Look at the sun, it's spinning," and he says, "So what else is new? Happens all the time here."

❦

Paintings of Mary through the centuries have depicted the significant events of her life, most of which are also recounted in the mysteries of the rosary, such as the Annunciation, the Visitation (to Elizabeth), Christ's birth, Simeon's prophecy, finding twelve-year-old Jesus in the temple, Mary's Dormition, Assumption, and Coronation. But probably the most common depiction is one in which Mary holds her baby, Jesus, in the crook of her left arm.

Some of the earliest of these mother-son images were not of Mary at all, but of Isis, the mother goddess of the Egyptians for three thousand years, and of the Greco-Roman world during Mary's time and after, who was depicted in exactly the same way. In the pagan world, people attributed miracles to icons, and the same is true of the Madonna and Child. The miracles, though, were almost exclusively performed by Mary and not by her son.

The miracle of Our Lady of Good Counsel was one such miracle. In the Middle Ages in the small town of Genazzano, in Latrium, Italy, a small church had begun to disintegrate, and a widow donated all her money to its renovation. But her money ran out before the reconstruction was complete, leaving one wall only half built, and as the town celebrated its feast day of Saint Mark, a cloud descended over the wall while a heavenly choir sang in the sky. Everyone looked up to see who was singing, but saw nothing until the cloud dissipated to reveal a portrait of the Virgin and Child resting on the unfinished wall.

A few days later, two Albanians arrived and claimed that the portrait was the same as the fresco that had disappeared from their church when the Turks invaded, a few days before. The portrait was exactly the measurement of the blank space left on the Albanian church's wall and was painted on plaster as thin as eggshells, too fragile to remove, let alone transport.

News of the miraculous painting spread fast, and people came from all over to worship the Madonna and Child. So many claimed cures and favors that a notary was directed to take down testimonies of the most striking cases. Between April and August of 1467, one hundred and seventy-one miracles were recorded.

The painting is inside a gold frame behind glass, but it touches neither and stands on its own, defying gravity. During World War II, a bomb destroyed the church's altar. A few feet away, the painting was untouched.

CHAPTER TWELVE

$\mathcal{M}$y last night in Medjugorje, before leaving for a tour of the miraculous sites of Italy, I take a shower, and as I towel myself dry, I wonder if I could ever become a nun and if becoming a nun would mean I could never again look at myself naked or touch my own body. As I look at myself naked in the mirror, I'm relieved that I don't seem to have gained weight from my diet of bread, and then I think that maybe when I fall in love the next time, my partner and I will not taste of each other's bodies until we're married. I figure I've never had much luck doing it the other way, and have been torturously conflicted about ever getting married at all. This way, if I want the intimacy and pleasure of sex, I'll have to get married—no choice, that simple. Maybe following the rules will make everything in life easier.

After I dress, I sit on my bed and study my hands. They're still raggedy and hideous, but feel fine. By the time they're done shedding the old blistered skin, every inch of surface will have peeled off. I wonder if I've been transformed: if new lines of identity really will be etched into the new skin on my palms. I think how hands are for caressing and applauding; hands fix things, they build, they help, they hold, they pray. What could Mary have been trying to tell me by giving me one of hers?

My miracle of the Mary statue has given me some fame among my fellow pilgrims. And as we stand in our long line at the airport in Split before departing for Rome, people become suddenly very interested in my hands. Jane, the Holy Roller doomsayer from Georgia, asks if she can please take a picture, because she's sure that when she develops them, she'll see words of prophecy etched in my palms, or maybe a picture of Mary.

But her camera won't click. A half-dozen more people try, and their cameras won't click, either. What does this mean? Again I'm being told to notice my hands. They were plagued by a torturously itchy rash. When I boarded the plane to Medjugorje, I was never for a second free of the urge to scratch them. As soon as I reached Medjugorje, the itch went away. An itch is like a longing. Maybe I won't be plagued by longing anymore. Maybe my heart has filled with love like I hoped it would, and there is no empty space left to fill. Maybe I'm being called to work on something, to do something. Maybe I'm supposed to become the first female priest. Maybe I'll join an order and write like Saint Therese of Lisieux—Therese the Little Flower, whom the lay Carmelite had said I reminded her of that night we'd told our stories at dinner.

Maybe Mary won't stop with new lines of identity; maybe I'll be blessed with a new brain, with which I'll deepen and expand Catholic theology—by incorporating quantum physics, say. One of the visionaries in Medjugorje had suddenly been able to speak Italian. Maybe as soon as we land in Italy, I'll be able to speak Italian, too.

I get a little carried away, but I'm relieved beyond imagination to believe truly that everything is possible with God.

Our first miraculous site is Maria Maggiore, which was built in the middle of the fourth century after Pope Liberius had a dream in which the Virgin appeared, telling him to build a church on one of the seven hills of Rome. The next morning, when he went to look at the hill Mary had shown him in the dream, he found it covered with snow in the shape of a cathedral. It was summer. Liberius took this as a sign and built the first cathedral to Mary in Rome.

Everywhere we go, I smell roses. On the streets in Rome. In Mary Major, in Saint Peter's Basilica, in my room. I'm not saying rosaries only en masse, but alone in my room, and it isn't laborious anymore. It keeps my mind focused on godly things, and focusing on godly things keeps me in a state of mild euphoria. I pray for peace in the world, and love. I concentrate on people I know and imagine Mary entering their hearts, spreading hope, making them feel love and reject despair; then I open the prayer to every person in the world. I pray for Jason, of course, only now I'm beginning to have faith that he really will heal.

Yet despite all this, I cannot bring myself to attend our audience with the Pope. I know he is a very holy and a very intelligent man. I know he has a special devotion to Mary and even credits her with saving his life when he was shot. I know he probably spends every moment of his life praying to God and probably even hearing God talking back. But he is strange about women. He is a man of a certain generation, born in a small Polish village, and he has not allowed his intelligence to overrule inherited opinions about the female sex, nor does he seem open enough to other religions. I find this intensely irritating and his stand against birth control beyond primitive. Plus, my gray roots are showing, so instead I have my hair dyed while the group stands among a thousand in Saint Peter's Square and receives the papal blessing.

After two days in Rome, we haul our luggage stuffed with statues and rosaries back to the bus and take off for a whirlwind trip of visits to the miraculous sites of southern-central Italy. Twelve miles from the Adriatic Sea, in San Luciano, we see the miracle of the Eucharist. Over twelve centuries ago, the congregation was entrusted to Brazilian monks. There was a monk among them "whose heart," it said in a video there, "was not grounded in faith but in supreme doubt. He was more dedicated to reason than contemplation." The monk doubted that during mass the Holy Eucharist literally was transformed into the body of Christ, which is essential Catholic doctrine, but believed that it was merely a symbol. During mass, while offering bread and wine, the bread in his hands turned into three-dimensional flesh and the wine turned into blood. At first the monk was frightened and confused; then his doubt turned into rapture. Tears of bliss streamed down his face, and he praised God for putting an end to his disbelief.

We climb up a short flight of stairs to look at the blackened host in a sepulcher and blood coagulated into what looks like a couple of small black rocks in a chalice. The video states that laboratory tests in 1971 positively identified the matter as flesh and blood belonging to the human species. In 1981 the flesh was further identified as endocardiac tissue. The last line of the video is "Not against reason but beyond it."

In San Giovanni Rotondo, Padre Pio's old parish, we're greeted by Father Joseph, a rotund, very effete priest in Franciscan robes with white hair and a white beard. "They're walkin' all over the place like ants," he frets about us in a Brooklyn accent. "Americans! Even if you voted for Clinton, you can come."

Father Joseph from Brooklyn brought us around the parish where Padre Pio, the stigmatist and charismatic, transubstantiating future saint, lived for sixty-five years. From the age of five in 1889, Padre Pio talked about giving himself to God. At sixteen he was accepted to study for the priesthood, and even before he left his little village Christ appeared to him. On one side were shining beautiful people, whom Christ identified as his children; on the other side were horrid monsters. Christ said to Pio, "You have to fight monsters to help my children. Don't worry. I'll be beside you."

Pio was sickly, and a month after he was ordained he was lying in the little hut he'd made of reeds, and Christ came, accompanied by Mary, and stigmatized Pio, opening wounds on Pio's hands, feet, and chest. But Pio was humble and didn't want people to make a big deal over him, so he asked the Lord to cover up the wounds but leave the pain. World War I broke out and Pio was drafted, but because he ran such high fevers and was so weak, he was given a medical discharge and two years to live. He lived fifty years longer.

Eight years passed. Pio said daily mass in the medieval church dedicated to the Virgin Mary. He was always in the Mary chapel praying. He called prayer "the sweet sleep" and "resting in the Holy Spirit." He said, "Pray, don't worry." Then, eight years after the stigmata first appeared, Christ appeared again. Rays of light shot from his wounds to Pio's, and the stigmata opened and bled. Pio again begged Christ to cover them up, but this time Christ said no. Pio hid his hands in his robes. Then one day his superior saw the red seeping through the robes and wanted to take a look. Pio broke down crying.

His superior sent him to a doctor, who poked his fingers through the holes in Pio's hands and feet and touched his thumb on the other side. It happened exactly the same way with the second and third doctors. Pio was the first priest to be a stigmatist. Saint Francis of Assisi, who also bore the stigmata, was a deacon and not a priest. There have been 333 stigmatists approved by the Church. Most are women. "Women can love God more than men," said Father Joseph from Brooklyn.

Every night Pio's wounds would cover with skin as thick as an orange's, and every morning the skin would peel off and the wounds would lie open. Pio wore gloves to hide his wounds except when he offered the Eucharist during mass. Word spread about the stigmatist priest and hordes of people trekked up the hill to San Giovanni Rotundo to take confession and communion with Padre Pio, who was busy morning, noon, and night, sleeping only two hours a day and surviving on the equivalent of a jar of baby food. Pio never took a day's vacation. The scent of roses was everywhere. Because there were so many people, after a while the padre hadn't enough time to sit in a confessional, so he would walk down a line of people, look each in his or her eyes, then kiss a cheek or touch a forehead, hit someone with his rope belt, completely ignore another, sensing what each needed to heal. Father Joseph told us how a woman came to confession, saw the padre, and exclaimed, "Oh, my God— you're the priest I confessed to in Brazil!" to which Pio responded, "That's right, and did you do what I said?" Padre Pio had the gift of bilocation and could be in two places at the same time, Father Joseph tells us.

We peer inside Pio's room, where, Father Joseph says, cries and thuds would often be heard in the night. Once Father Joseph himself ran into the cell and saw Pio being thrown around the room, and as Pio lay on the floor bruised, a pillow floated from a chair to the floor, then under his head. Later Pio told how Satan had come to beat him up, as he often did, and that Our Lady had appeared to comfort him and had placed the pillow under his head. "Padre Pio had great devotion to Our Lady."

Father Joseph leads us into a room with a mound of books and rosaries for sale, as well as Pio medals with little pieces of Pio's garments under a bubble of clear plastic. An elderly priest I've recognized from pictures in some of the books as Pio's close companion bows before each of us and offers us tea as Father Joseph says, "Would you all like a blessing?" Choruses of yeses. He reaches into a drawer and pulls out a Baggie containing a blood-encrusted glove. "Padre Pio's," he says, then walks around the room, touching the glove to each of our foreheads. I feel heat shoot down to my toes, and tears of gratefulness, surrender, sweet release— call them tears of bliss—flow and flow. These are the same tears I've been weeping in church at Medjugorje and every day after. My heart is filled with the feeling of just stepping foot in my home after being away for a lifetime.

Every day, I cry several times, and always when I say the words before communion, "Lord I am not worthy to receive you, but only say the word and I shall be healed." It's bliss really, a draining of my defenses, a softening and an opening, and so much gratefulness to Mary. The weeping itself leaves me peaceful and euphoric. Father Joseph says that Pio had the gift of tears and could fill jars with the water that fell from his eyes. I think I have this gift, too.

I do not, however, have the gift of good feelings for my fellow man. In fact, my fellow pilgrims are beginning to grate on my nerves. They've begun to revert to their old, less angelic selves as the heaven we tasted in Medjugorje begins to fade. Day after day, we squeeze into a bus in which every seat is filled and from which, every evening, we have to lug our ever-growing luggage—we amass more and more icons at every stop. Day after day a percentage of us has had to contend with trying to buy water or soda or chocolate at a roadside store only to find everyone else has bought out the supply of water or soda or chocolate. The mountain roads are narrow and winding, producing motion sickness in at least half of us. So, we scramble for seats at the front of the bus, where the oceanic weaving of our vehicle is less severe. I have a long history of selfishness, and so am a master right from the beginning at jockeying myself into a position to score a good seat; but as the days wear on, my fellow pilgrims get savvier and more selfish, until they resort to thievery. Once when I reenter the bus after leaving it for a moment at a rest stop, someone has stolen my seat.

We arrive in Assisi, our last stop, a few weeks after a devastating earthquake has virtually collapsed the basilica. We are not allowed inside but are entertained by another American Franciscan, leaning on a cane, outside the doors. Father Andrew tells us how Saint Francis was from a wealthy family, and how when given the choice between marriage and war, he had chosen war. He was captured in France and thrown into a dungeon, where he almost died; his father ransomed him, and when Francis finally came home he recovered his health slowly. His family worried because he was so changed, and had even been seen talking to birds. (He eventually became the patron saint of animals.) Saint Francis took to heart Christ's words:

Look at the birds of the air; they neither sow nor reap nor gather into barns, and yet your heavenly Father feeds them. And are you not of more value than they? And can any of you by worrying add a single hour to your life? And why do you worry about clothing? Consider the lilies of the field, how they grow;

they neither toil nor spin, yet I tell you, even Solomon in all his glory was not clothed like one of these. But if God clothes the grass of the field, which is alive today and tomorrow is thrown into the oven, will he not much more clothe you—you of little faith. Therefore do not worry, saying, "What will we eat?" or "What will we drink?" or "What will we wear?"

Saint Francis cast off his clothes and found an abandoned chapel near Assisi that he began to rebuild with his bare hands, saying to people, "For every brick you give me, God will give you two." He was reviled by the townspeople, but some of his old friends joined him, and eventually Francis founded the Franciscan order, which requires hard work and a vow of poverty. Two years before he died he was stigmatized, and after that he was repeatedly attacked by Satan. Father Slavko had said that Satan was tirelessly working against good, and that saints and mystics were tortured by him, because wherever there is much good Satan will come and try to work his evil. "Our Lady is our first exorcist," he said. On one of his visits, Satan threw Saint Francis into the rosebushes, and the thorns disappeared.

We see the thornless roses.

"You can be like Saint Francis," Father Andrew says. "All you have to do is love God and love your neighbor as yourself. You can be rich—God bless you—just don't put anything between you and God."

That night, our last, Father Freed conducts a healing mass in the chapel in our motel. And for two hours before, he gives confessions in a little room adjoining the chapel.

Nearly every one of the pilgrims wants to go to confession, so it seems like an eternity before I get in to see the father. I confess how much everyone is annoying me. I tell him how this big fat guy sat behind me and poked his knees into my seat for the entire trip to Assisi and how I had to restrain myself from turning around and throwing food at him, but wasn't able to restrain myself from intentionally blocking his exit from his seat with my luggage for as long as I could manage it. "I just get so annoyed. It's hard to feel love. It's hard to like people. The first thing that comes to my mind is the criticism, the fault."

"A lot of us have been feeling this. I want you to try to follow any criticism with something to praise."

I picture that big guy who annoyed me the most. He's a blowhard, his wife can't get a word in edgewise, and he *knew* he was ramming his knee into my back through the seat. What can I possibly think of to praise him for?

"That's really hard, Father Freed," I say. "I don't know if I'll be able to."

"I want you to promise to try."

I remember that our first night in Rome, one of the women had thought her bag had been stolen from her room, and this man had taken it upon himself to talk to the manager and to accompany the woman to the police. It turned out to be a false alarm, but he had been the one to help and to feel responsible for the safety of the rest of us. That certainly was something to praise. "And Beverly," Father Freed continues, "tonight during the services I want you to try to be open to the Holy Spirit."

"I will."

After mass, Father Freed calls Bruce and one of the single men, Fred, who's from Father Freed's congregation in Iowa, to come to the altar. Then, as we sing "Come, Holy Spirit," we walk one by one up to Father Freed in front of the altar. I watch as Father Freed presses the palm of his hand to people's foreheads and they fall like trees into Bruce's and Fred's hands. I begin to sweat. Father Freed is going to press his palm to my forehead and chances are good that I'm going to faint. Everybody else is. But something inside me resists. I'm the cynic again, the outsider, unable to join. I don't want to be slain in the spirit like the others. But my feet carry me forward and I approach the altar, my face pouring sweat.

In front of Father Freed, my heart beating so hard my breathing becomes shallow, I close my eyes, think, "Come, Holy Spirit," and as Father Freed presses his hand to my forehead, I feel wobbly and vertiginous, but pleasantly so. I decide I can resist and remain standing, and in control, or I can surrender, let myself go, see what it feels like. I let myself go and fall backwards in a divine falling-down swoon, like a baby who's never been dropped. Then I am caught by four strong hands and eased to the floor, where I lie till the wave of bliss washes through me.

❧

I can't begin to tell you all the stories I know about statues of the Virgin Mary in which she was found and either refused to move, or was placed in a cart and pulled by a donkey—or car-

ried by a monk—and at a certain location she suddenly became so heavy, it was impossible to move forward. And so they let her stay where she chose, and a shrine, followed by a chapel, then a church, and sometimes even a cathedral, was built to house her.

Mary statues with this kind of self-determination were powerful and worked miracles for those who came to worship and ask for favors. Some of these statues date as far back as the fourth century. Through time, Mary's place in the countryside may have been overtaken by Saracens or Turks or some other heathen who tried to carry her off or harm her, and the hapless heathen ended up writhing in pain on the ground, his arm fell off, or he dropped dead. His companions might have then burned down the church, and Mary survived unscorched.

There are stories of the devout follower who thought Mary worthy of a more beautiful or accessible abode and so carried her there, only to find the next morning that the Virgin had made her way back to the home she had chosen for herself, sometimes with mud on her skirt.

CHAPTER THIRTEEN

*O*n my way home, I pushed my seat on the plane into its reclining position, pulled down the window shade, and as I was about to doze off I was brought back by a memory of a Mary statue that stands on top of the cathedral in Loreto, Italy. Loreto is a town built around Mary's humble little house, which the angels are said to have flown from Nazareth to Italy. A slightly more believable story goes that the Crusaders carried it brick by brick (the bricks actually do date back to Mary's time) when Nazareth was invaded by Muslims. As you approach Loreto the first thing you see, standing on top of the cathedral's spire, is Mary, outlined in tiny white lights, illuminating the sky. It had felt so right, so downright safe, to have the Mother all lit up, the first, last, and highest presence in the sky, that I had a fantasy: What if we could see Mary looking down on Los Angeles?

Back in LA, driving the freeway, I felt like I was in love; all I could think about was Mary. I was consumed, obsessed. It felt the same as, say, getting to know a man by being around him for a long time, then realizing you are actually attracted.

He begins to enter your mind at odd moments. He's the last thing you think of before bed and the first thing you think of in the morning. You walk through your day looking at things through his eyes. He's called you a few times, maybe he's even asked you out; but you don't know if he's asked you just as a friend. And then, one glorious evening, across the table at dinner, or just as you break away from a slow dance, he says, "I am so in love with you." You flood with a delicious tickly excitement and a warm peaceful relief at the same time.

That's how I felt about Mary. I could not get the Blessed Mother out of my mind; she was in my heart; she was the air I breathed. I wanted to give her gifts, to tell everyone who and what I'd found.

But at dinner with my closest women friends on Saturday night, I was careful not to let them know the depth of my passion, or to proselytize. I did want them to know I pray to Mary, so that over time when they saw the change in me, they too might begin praying, and who knows, open their hearts, let Mary take their hands, find peace, and be less afraid. After I told my miracle stories, I experienced a twinge of my old, customary everybody-thinks-I'm-an-idiot moment, and shook it off. Mary loved me; I must be lovable.

For the first time in my life, I understood why people proselytize: you are happy, you have found a way, you want to share it so others may find it, too. But I controlled it, handed my gifts of gold and silver rosaries around the table, and with restraint said, "These were blessed by Mary. I know, I know—it's hard to believe. But they have power.

Just keep the beads near you. Put them under your pillow. You may wake up in the middle of the night and want to pray. Or just say a Hail Mary." They seemed to think that they might.

Jason flew in to LA to see some friends. We made a date to meet at a West Hollywood bar with a pool table. I sat on a bar stool, watching Jason sink expert shots, waiting for an opportunity to present him with his wooden rosary beads, a silver medal of Our Lady of Peace that looks just like the statue with the broken hand, a white pressed-marble crucifix, and a Saint Benedict's medal I suggested he could use as a key chain: "It keeps away evil." He smiled and said, "Cool," which gave me hope that he wouldn't just stick them in a drawer.

I wanted to tell him about my heart, how sorry I was, how I prayed for him, but it would have to wait, because it was impossible to arrange a time to be alone with him.

I decided to visit the Virgin of Guadalupe on her feast day, December 12, in her basilica in Mexico City, built on the spot where she appeared to Juan Diego in 1531. As Father Freed suggested for my penance, I would ask Guadalupe to help me forgive myself for my abortion.

Meanwhile, I resumed my yoga classes three mornings a week and went to my office every day to begin reading some books I'd collected about Mary. I didn't even have to look at my watch to know when it was time for mass. The bells at Saint Augustine's across Washington Boulevard rang and I felt a pull on my chest and knew viscerally for the first time why churches ring bells: to call you home. As soon as they tolled I knew I had ten minutes to get myself over there. I don't remember noticing those bells before Medjugorje.

At the noon mass, a tiny hunchbacked lady in turquoise slacks and smudged white sneakers, named Dottie, would begin a rosary, "a rosary to Our Lady for world peace," she would announce as the priest left the altar and the people filed from their pews. Sometimes as few as six gathered round Dottie, sometimes as many as thirty. Sometimes I prayed, sometimes I just sat behind and did my twenty-minute meditation to the chanting of their Hail Marys; sometimes I left. A few times I led a decade.

The congregation was a mixture of Latinos, whites, Filipinos. Church was the only place in LA where I mingled with people who were different from me. We daily church-goers sat in the same seat every day, and there was a comfort in the predictability of this. When the priest said, "Show one another a sign of peace," I shook hands with the same people every day, saying, "Peace be with you."

To touch people I didn't know, to look in their eyes and smile, to sincerely wish them peace, to receive a wish of peace from them, the plain goodness in this warmed me to the bone, and tears filled my eyes almost every time.

I fasted on bread and water on Wednesdays and Fridays (I'd asked Father Freed if I could change it to a juice fast for the sake of good health and he'd said no). I prayed my three rosaries (on my way to work, on my way home, and in bed at night), but most of the time I was disappointed in, even disgusted with, the priests, especially a particularly good-looking young one I soon learned to avoid at Saint Augustine's. In an attempt to let us know that he was just a regular guy, not so different from the rest of us, during his homily, nine times out of ten, he managed to fit in a mention of how "I was Rollerblading the other day"—followed by some lame observation like, "and I remembered the knock-knock jokes. Remember—'Knock knock,' 'Who's there?' Well, praying is a little like that. If you knock, God always answers. Thank you." I knew, as a good Catholic, I was not supposed to criticize priests, but with a priest like this it was hard not to snort, especially when he winked at a beautiful young girl as he walked back down the aisle after Sunday mass and said, "Smile."

I searched all over LA for a good priest, but in the end I needn't have looked any farther than my own office backyard, because I never found a priest I liked as well as Father Michael Santori, also of Saint Augustine's. Santori was my age, portly, a composer, and like most artists, a little crazy. On occasion, caught up in his homily, he let slip a mention of his therapist. He knew Scripture and history. He loved God and Jesus, who, as far as I understood it, were one and the same—and so was the Holy Spirit. It's all so confusing, and I loved it for that. Reason had done nothing to take away the misery in my life; I was only too happy to leave reason at the church's door.

I read that there were those in the Church who believed

the Holy Spirit was Mary. It was the Holy Spirit that lit the little flames on the heads of the apostles: inspiration, awareness, faith. It was Mary who'd lit the little flame for me.

Faith was Father Michael's favorite subject. The first homily I heard him give was after the reading in the Bible where Jesus returns to his hometown and has trouble performing miracles because people have so little faith. Father Michael walked to the top of the aisle and said, "'Amazed' is not a good word in the Bible. The apostles were always amazed. They didn't get it. If you are amazed, then you don't have enough faith, and without faith you won't have God. Remember Peter walked on water until he stopped for a moment, couldn't believe he was doing it, got scared, and started to go under? 'You of little faith, why did you doubt?' Christ said. If you don't have faith, it's impossible for God to show himself. Jesus went back to his hometown. He was the carpenter's son; who was he to proclaim such powers? Who was he to perform miracles? And so because they didn't believe in him, he could do nothing. Your heart has to be open for God to come in."

I tried to keep my heart open, and on the plane to Mexico City to see the Virgin of Guadalupe, I asked God to show me his will, then pictured Mary leading me by the hand. The last time I'd been to Mexico, I'd been in love with Kip, the only man I'd thought I'd spend the rest of my life with. That had been nine years ago, and I hadn't been in love since. Just smelling the Mexican air could trigger unwanted romantic memories and throw me into a pit of despair in which I would believe I'd never find love again.

Everywhere I went, Mexican men asked, "You are alone? Where is your husband? Have you no children?" I felt like an aberration of nature; I even considered wrapping a baby doll in a shawl and posing as a mother. I had rented a room in the historic center of town and took a stroll my first evening, weaving through the street vendors crowding the sidewalks. I felt something poke my behind ever so slightly and dipped into a doorway to let whomever had bumped me pass. As I did, I looked at the person. It was a young man holding a huge penis. "That's *disgusting*! You fucking *asshole*!" I screamed at the top of my lungs. The boy's face fell and he looked as if he might cry. For a second I felt sorry for him. I went back to the hotel and turned on the television. But that huge penis loomed too large to concentrate—some sign I should interpret? How did it make me feel? More alone.

The celebration of Guadalupe's day actually begins the night before, when a string of performers starting at seven in the evening serenade La Virgen. The big show, anticipated by the entire country, begins at eleven, with Mexico's biggest musical stars performing in an extravaganza; then, at midnight, there is a mass. The whole thing is broadcast on TV and watched all over Mexico. One million people were expected at the basilica. I was falling in love with Mexico because it so loved Mary.

I decided I would arrive at the festivities at five to be ensured a seat. I was very worried about having to go to the bathroom, which was highly likely, not just once during the evening but two or three or four times. I would be sitting there for at least eight hours. Then what would happen to my seat? And where would the bathrooms be, how long the lines, and how disgusting? I said a Hail Mary, remembering Padre Pio's dictum "Pray, don't worry."

The basilica was like New Year's Eve at Times Square times two. Groups with outfits that looked like running suits with the names of their towns and CLUB GUADALUPANA written in a circle on their backs came from all over Mexico. Many of them were walking or riding bikes; others crowded onto the backs of trucks. Old ladies walked on their knees up the avenue to the basilica. People carried VIVA LA VIRGEN banners and had strapped huge Guadalupe pictures on their backs. They held them aloft as they marched down the middle aisle of the cathedral, which had been left open for this purpose, a constant stream of Mary worshipers thirty people wide and a hundred people deep. They stopped only to kneel at the front of the line while two priests with tireless arms sprinkled them with holy water. As it grew dark outside and the crowd denser, smoke billowed into the air and a deep, loud drumming rumbled like a threatening earthquake. It did not feel holy and peaceful but pagan and scary. I was grateful for my inside seat.

A woman, who was probably younger than I but looked like she was sixty, sat next to me with two little girls, around two and three. The smaller one had on a turquoise dress with white patent-leather shoes and lacy socks, all dirty. The girl cried, not loudly but piteously, her body shaking and tears shiny on her cheeks. Every once in a while she'd see me looking at her and force a wide toothy smile while still crying. What would it be like to have that child, to pick her up and soothe her? The woman in front gave her a roll; the woman in back, a cookie. Her sister patted her head, but it did no good. Finally, after a few hours, she stopped. I gave her a piece of paper and a pencil and she drew. Then she climbed over me and crawled under the pew into the next aisle. The mother never once seemed the slightest bit annoyed. She brought out their dinner, which was sweet rolls, and wrapped the little girl in her rebozo, cradled her in her arms, and tried to get her to sleep. I thought how courageous that woman was to be alone amid this mob with two little children, to come out on this night with her girls to honor the Virgin.

Performer after performer, their backs to the audience, facing the painting of the Virgin of Guadalupe, sang their hearts out—campesinos all in white, down on one knee, their sombreros over their hearts; choruses of girls in Catholic-school uniform singing "Ave Maria"; mariachi bands in their studded pants crooning in their whiny plaintive voices. And then, shortly before eleven, three hundred priests filed into seats on the huge horseshoe-shaped altar, and a performance that could have been the finale of the Ice Capades began. With the last bombastic strains of the serenading, I realized we were going to have mass, and those three hundred priests were going to attempt to give communion to a million-plus people. The Blessed Mother would certainly love for me to stay and have communion, but I was too cowardly. There would be a mass exodus after it. It was already past midnight, and it might take till two to fight my way to a holy host. At the homily, I made my exit, squeezing myself down the aisle and out of the church, then joining first one stream, then another, a moving current through the ocean of people. I had no idea in which direction I should be walking, so I just followed the crowds. Two hours and a few miles later, I was able to flag a cab to my hotel. For the first time in ten hours, I needed to relieve my bladder. A miracle.

The next day, I visited Morelia, the lovely colonial town where Kip and I drove every week to shop and go to a movie. It was in the Morelia cathedral that I'd sat and wept for the first time about my aborted baby. I wanted to reclaim the place. I wanted Mexico back in my life, and not have it be defined by my failure, not be redolent with hurt. I'd never planned to stay away from Mexico for so long. As I walked the streets and revisited the market, I remembered what I had felt like back then, being part of a couple, and could feel a hole opening back up in me, one I'd thought I'd filled with Mary, filled for good.

The center aisle in the cathedral was lined with huge bouquets of white roses in celebration of Guadalupe. I sat and closed my eyes, remembering when I'd lived near this cathedral. I thought of Labor Day, 1989, almost ten years ago, and how I'd finished my first book and mailed it to my publisher, then threw all the previous drafts in the garbage. Then Kip and I left town to celebrate. We drove five hours to San Miguel de Allende, which is Mexico's equivalent of the Hamptons; its nickname is Gringolandia. We counted the things we could do there: drink cappuccino, have ice in a drink without worrying about the turista, hear jazz, dance salsa, maybe even (dare we dream it?) eat a hamburger. Kip had been working harder than usual, and I was due back in New York to research a magazine article. The weekend was a combination vacation, farewell-till-we-meet-again-stateside-at-Christmas, and celebration because I'd finally finished my book.

It was late in the day on Saturday when we brought our bags into the hotel room. I wanted to look through the shops at all the tin and ceramics, but Kip didn't want to shop. So we arranged to meet at a restaurant at eight-thirty. I looked through a few shops and bought some tin Christmas ornaments, then went to meet Kip.

La Fragua was down some stairs, where candlelit tables surrounded a courtyard. I took a table toward the back and watched a large group of ten or so young Mexicans in front of me. By the stylish way they were dressed I guessed they were weekending from Mexico City. Three men with guitars stood on a little platform in the middle of the courtyard and began playing Beatles songs. I ordered a margarita and leaned back, taking it all in.

By the time Kip arrived, apologizing for getting tied up, looking at some horse farm on the outskirts of town, I was on my third margarita. Kip sat and ordered his own margarita and smiled at the beautiful Mexican women in front of us, not at me. I waited for him to look at me, which did not happen till he opened the menu and said, "You know what you want?"

I couldn't stop myself. "Did you kiss another woman before I came to Mexico?" I asked.

I couldn't bring myself to say "sleep with," "fuck," or "make love to." If he answered yes, I would die.

Kip put on a look of forced patience. "Beverly," he said, "don't ask questions you don't want to hear the answers to."

"YOU DID."

"You really do not want to have this discussion."

"Yes I do."

"Where's this coming from? Because I didn't want to go shopping?"

"YOU DID."

"I finally have time to relax, take a little vacation, to feel romantic, and you ask that question now?"

"And when would it be right? Back at home at breakfast? When I first arrived in Mexico? I never asked before because I thought it would be insulting. I can't believe it. You kissed someone."

"It was nothing. It was only once. I wasn't going to stay home seven nights a week for six months. The guys go out and dance. That's what I did. I danced, I talked to girls. I never took a phone number or saw a girl again. One night I kissed someone. No big deal."

"I wanted you to be mine." I was barely audible. I collapsed on his shoulder in tears.

"Bev . . ." He stroked my head. "It was innocent. I didn't sleep with her. It meant nothing."

I removed my head from his shoulder.

"Look. Give me some credit. I told you the truth. I didn't have to. There was a lot of temptation."

"And now I'm leaving again. And you're going to go dancing and kissing girls?"

"No, I won't. I swear to you. Besides, you don't have to go. I can support you."

"I have a career." I would not allow a man to support me again, and I'd committed to writing a story about a high school for pregnant and parenting teenage girls on Long Island. Besides, Mexico was Kip's thing, not mine. "You danced with a beautiful woman all night." The image was so richly torturous I couldn't let it go.

"Why are you doing this?"

"I don't trust you."

"Fine."

I ordered ravioli in a red cream sauce made with vodka and didn't eat it. Back in our hotel room, we made love and it was shamefully delicious. As I fell asleep, I wondered where my anger had really come from. I decided I was going to try to be adult about Kip's flirting. Or European. It was only a kiss. I would let it go.

In the morning, I was awakened by a brass band and the church bells clanging riotously. I figured it must be a religious feast, because there was a religious feast every other week in Mexico.

Kip said he'd join me when he was more awake, and I walked down to the central plaza to see what was happening. In procession in front of a truck, men wearing white campesino outfits with sombreros beat drums, while others in feathered headdresses and clacking seed pods, tied in clusters to their ankles, hopped and twirled in circles. In the truck bed stood a statue of the Blessed Virgin holding a bleeding heart. She was dressed in white edged with gold. Her deep-brown hair was long and thick. The truck went round and round the central garden, the statue wobbling in back. I moved a little closer. The Virgin's eye blinked. Oh, my God—the Virgin Mary was not a statue but a live young woman tied to a rod, posing as a statue, and the heart she held was real.

I had no curiosity about the life of the real young woman posing as Mary. What interested me was that a woman could look so like a statue, and that a statue could actually be a woman—that Mary could look artificial and be real, be real but look artificial. This woman statue in the bed of that truck suddenly seemed the sum of all I'd secretly known about the Virgin all along: a heart beat just beneath the surface; a real tear could drop at any moment; one's own image could be reflected in the pupil of her eye.

For a moment I felt as I did when I was a child and had fallen asleep in the car. I'd wake up as my father lifted me and I'd feel a flutter in my heart, so thrilled to be nestled against my father's chest, safe and warm and bobbing in the sky, hoping he would never put me back down.

That Sunday evening, as we drove back home down the potted dirt road to our village, I saw something white tangled in the trees. As we drove closer I realized it was my book—all my drafts on the long scroll of paper I'd thrown in the dump. Some kids had no doubt run with it—a long dragon tail behind them, twisting over bushes, wrapping round fences, hanging from trees. My book—the memoir that had been so important to me, the result of all the sacrifices and choices I'd made to be able to accomplish it, the thousands of words I'd thought defined me—had actually given pleasure and left its mark. Somehow it seemed appropriate that my "mark" looked like a roll of toilet paper attacked by a litter of kittens.

As I sat in the cathedral in Morelia, smelling the sweet roses with my eyes closed, it seemed to me that Mary had been appearing to me all of my life, more than I'd ever noticed. I had taken home with me the Guadalupe throw that covered my computer in Mexico. It had been the first Mary in my Orient house.

I'd gone looking for Mary because I felt unloved and unlovable and was filled with an unquenchable longing. I'd hoped that if I could feel the love of God, or Mary, the longing would stop. I'd hoped that once God filled me with love, it would overflow onto others.

Back when I lived in Mexico, I did not believe that Kip loved me. I never believed any man loved me—after Ray. I didn't trust him, and I anticipated the worst. And that's what I got. When Kip came back, a few months later, to live with me in the States, I discovered he'd been having an affair with a twenty-four-year-old virgin. I'd left him and moved to Orient. It was the worst hurt, because it was the last time I'd been hurt by love, and this hurt carried the weight of every disappointment I'd had in love in my life. I'd suffered deeply, and it was only then, in my desperation, that I was able to let Mary in.

After I left the cathedral, I called the veterinarian who'd been Kip's sponsor and sort of a friend.

"Come to my house," Guillermo said.

As we sat down for *comida* with his son Raúl, who'd been fifteen when I last saw him and was now twenty-four, Guillermo said, "You just missed Kip. He was here for his daughter's baptism."

I must have turned white, because Guillermo said, "You knew he married. . . ."

I'd heard from one of Kip's college friends that Kip had married the woman he'd been seeing while he was still with me. They lived first in a trailer in Texas, where he'd been the vet at a game preserve; then they'd moved to Africa, where Kip ran another wild-game preserve.

"We went to the celebration at her family's," Raúl said.

"How did Kip look?" I asked, but what I wanted to know was, Is he happy? I wanted to be a good Christian and to want happiness for him, but I wasn't sure I was being sincere.

"He looked good. The same," said Guillermo.

Raúl drove me back to my hotel, and I invited him for a beer on the terrace. Raúl told me that he was quitting his job in a couple of months to travel for a year. He said it was difficult for him because his friends were all Mexican (Raúl had a German mother) and didn't understand. They were only twenty-four and most were already married with children or engaged. They didn't know that there was a whole world out there, that they could travel and see things, have adventures; all they knew was what they'd been exposed to: family. "Look at Kip," he said. "His wife cries all the time. He has to bring her home once a year."

I saw it all clearly. Nothing was simple. Nobody had it easy. His wife, who had always wanted to be a mother, but had thought her life would be one way, living near her mother and aunts and cousins, sharing in raising her family, speaking the language she grew up speaking, was in Africa with her husband. For all I knew she spoke only Spanish and Kip went off every day as he had with me and left her alone. Kip had a wife who was unhappy.

A weight lifted. Even for Kip things weren't perfect. Father Slavko's words about focusing on what we don't have came to mind. Perhaps I'd wanted to be alone. Perhaps I'd needed to be. I wouldn't have gone looking for Mary any other way.

When Jason was young and I hadn't the choice all those years, I'd been envious of anyone who traveled. This year, I'd been all over the U.S., to Bosnia, Italy, and now Mexico, thanks to Mary.

I forgave myself for failing with Kip, for pushing him away. I forgave Kip, too.

Conversion is a lifelong process; I'd only just begun, really, and it is work. Back home in LA, the religious disciplines began to dwindle until I ate anything I wanted on Wednesdays and Fridays; I said one daily rosary, not three. I still meditated, and went to mass on Sundays, but only occasionally to daily mass. I did, however, make an effort to be open to Jesus, because I knew Mary would want this. I read a book of parallel sayings of the Christ and the Buddha, and a wonderful, smart book called *Meeting Jesus for the First Time Again,* and I was riveted by Mary's son. Jesus was a radical thinker, an amazing storyteller, poet, holy man, and revolutionary. He was killed because he would not back down from what he knew was the truth. I loved him for getting on that donkey and riding into town. I'd come to believe that the Father, the Son, the Holy Spirit, and Mary, too, were all different faces of God, or love, or an impulse toward good in the world. It helped me to see the Spirit as people. I pictured them all at different times when I prayed, and some saints, too. But I responded most strongly to a woman. A mother was what I desired; a mother and all "mother" means—softness, gentle care, compassion—was what the world needed, too. And so Mary remained my focus.

It seemed to me that God or the Spirit or Mary speaks to you in many different ways, usually indirectly, sometimes through other people, sometimes through signs. But you have to pay attention; mostly God speaks to you in a whisper, so you have to be silent to hear. It was so much richer to go through life listening in this way, and looking for signs.

When I went to mass during the week some time near Easter, Father Michael mentioned at the beginning that after mass there would be a ceremony having to do with the cross. I was tired and was not going to stay. The cross, he said in his homily, is the truth, the truth that Christ preached. It is hard to face the truth, but you must not only face it, you must embrace it: the truth about oneself, about one's own weaknesses and especially one's fears, as well as the truth that Christ preached as the Good News and the Way.

I tried to process this: Christ chose his own martyrdom to call attention to his truth. Christ died so that the truth would be remembered through his death. I wondered if saying that Christ died for our sins is the same as saying he died telling us what sin was, and so he died so we would know how *not* to sin.

The symbolism was so rich. Just as when we are born we know we will die, Christ's Resurrection was present in his death. Release is present in suffering. Pain is the raw material for joy.

I was no theologian, but realized that as time went on, as I continued to meditate and to read, my understanding would deepen. I was not impatient. This study, I hoped, would hold a fascination for me till I died.

But this evening I was tired and did not want to stay to venerate the cross. As soon as Father Michael served the last communicant, I stood to leave, but then something made me sit back down. I was no longer comfortable with my old self, who thought I knew best what I needed. I had already sat through an entire mass when I hadn't really felt like it; I could certainly exert a little more effort and stay. I would do this for Mary, and for her son—a little sacrifice.

And I was rewarded. Father Michael wheeled a ten-foot-high cross down the center aisle. Then, pew by pew, we all stood in line to touch it, and as I stood there with these strange but not strange people, I had what I was beginning to think of as that religious feeling—that somber joy, that glad sadness, that rush of rich, deep funny-bone gratefulness—and as I touched the cross, my blissful tears poured.

These symbolic gestures, the stained glass, the flickering candles, the chanting, the bells, the incense made me believe I might stay devout throughout my life. It was also the sweet tears that continued to flow, and the heat in my heart when I received the host, the delicious feelings of humility, gratefulness, love that came to me so easily here.

Soon after that Easter, Father Santori was transferred out of the parish, and no one came even close to replacing him. I gave dinner parties, I met friends for movies, talked about casting the movie of *Riding in Cars with Boys,* went to the museum with my friend Namik. I was comfortable in my life, but there was a flatness to it, too. In Los Angeles, everything seemed like an act. I'd been to a movie premiere where there was a swing band, and the swing band seemed like it was "playing" a swing band. Nothing seemed authentic; nothing seemed to be simply itself. Everything seemed to be an imitation. I'd noticed this before, but now it had begun to alienate me—especially when the priest who replaced Father Michael showed up on *NYPD Blue* "playing" the priest who gave Jimmy Smits his last rites.

Then, one day at the end of July, nine months after I came home from Medjugorje, I received an e-mail from a friend I'd met ten years ago in Mexico in San Miguel de Allende. He lives half the time there and half in LA. Tony wrote about the acres of gladiolus at the covered market, the Indian ladies selling tortillas and cactus and pomegranate.

He reminded me of the sonorous church bells that ring from every direction, and said, "Why don't you come down?"

What I heard was: Mary's here.

Still, my immediate reaction was, it's too much of a stretch. I was on a writing deadline. I might be distracted. And where would I stay? But a feeling in my gut shouted, "Go! Mary will help." And five days later I was on a plane.

❦

Christ said in Luke: "For nothing is hidden that will not be disclosed, nor is anything secret that will not become known."

❦

CHAPTER FOURTEEN

Mary was everywhere. There are two covered markets in San Miguel, and Guadalupe is enshrined in each one; she is on the facades of private homes; she is in the public fountains; there are an average of four Marys in each of the fifty churches; and, incredibly, "Ave Maria" is played on the local radio station every noon. In my opinion, although Roman Catholicism purports to be monotheistic, it is really polytheistic, and Mexicans make no bones about it. Mary is more prominent than Jesus. And Mary is worshiped in each of her many manifestations, mainly as Guadalupe, the strong and loving protectress of the disenfranchised, the lowly, the people with dark skin. Mary is like the Statue of Liberty. Mary is the Mother of Mexico.

Of the fifty churches to walk to every day, the one I visited most was La Salud, which was the small church next to the grand church that contained the duplicate of Mary's house in Loreto (but because this was Mexico, the little humble house of Mary was lined in gold). English mass every Sunday is offered in Mary's house.

At La Salud, Mary behind the altar is Mary as Glinda the Good Witch. She wears sky blue trimmed in gold. Her hair is blond corkscrew curls and her face is, I swear, Glinda's. In her left hand she holds out her baby, Jesus, in all his blond Son of Good Witch glory. As you walk in, you pass another Mary in a painting in a glass box. She has darker hair and is standing in the flames of hell, lifting people up. Left noticeably behind is a bishop wearing a grand red hat. But the real draw of La Salud is Niño Santo, a child Jesus, who stands inside a glass case in an alcove to the left of the altar. He holds some sort of medal in his hand, and inside of his glass case are hundreds of little toys and *milagros*—metal replicas of body parts. On the walls surrounding the glass case are hundreds of casts and pictures and letters of gratitude for healings that have occurred—thanks, people believe, to the prayers they sent to Niño Santo.

Standing next to the Niño, in the corner, is Mary as Dolorosa. It is Glinda's face exactly, only older. Her hair is darker and her cheeks are shiny with tears. She is wearing purple velvet and her hands are clasped at her heart; a few *milagros* are pinned to her skirt.

I sat many days in that corner. I meditated, I prayed the rosary. Because I often prayed as I walked the streets, I was now adept at counting off the Hail Marys on my fingers— and I asked Niño Santo and Mary to help me with my son. I slipped a *milagro* of a heart I'd bought at Guadalupe's basilica under the glass and into Niño Santo's box, then knelt and prayed: "Help my son heal. Help me forgive myself," I asked for possibly the one thousandth time.

I'd tried to strike up an e-mail correspondence from Mexico with Jason, but he didn't respond. When I persisted in writing him anyway, he finally wrote back, attacking me. He didn't trust me, he said. Writing was too easy. Words meant nothing, especially from me. I remembered that he'd been angry at me when I moved to Mexico with Kip. He'd been a junior in college. Back then, I'd told him I'd call from the border, but then forgot. I thought he was probably reacting to that time. But whom was I kidding? There were so many of those times to react to. So much anger there. He asked me not to write him.

Finally, my worst fear had come true. My son wanted nothing to do with me.

Back in the States it was fall and things began to happen: I went to visit a TV writer friend who had not been "arrested" that season—the Hollywood term for hired to write on a TV show. I'd brought her a rosary souvenir from Medjugorje, and as I handed it to her she said, "Oh, my God, I can't believe this." Just the day before, she'd looked up how to say the rosary on the Internet, and had told Mary that if Mary wanted her to pray, then Mary would have to make a rosary appear. I gave another friend her rosary and she too said "I can't believe it": "I just said a Hail Mary this morning for the first time in twenty years." Another friend, whose father had had a heart attack, told me that she'd just been to mass, and that as she sat there, she'd wished for a rosary.

So many of my friends, it seemed, had reason to pray. And

so did I. I prayed constantly: as I walked on the beach, as I drove in my car, first thing when I opened my eyes in the morning and last thing before I fell asleep at night. I prayed for my son: that he would heal.

I planned my trip back east for Christmas. I called Jason and told him I'd be in New York for three weeks and asked if he'd consider going to therapy with me, twice a week, six times. He agreed. We found a family therapist through Jason's therapist. The plan was that we would each meet with her alone once and then go to her together the remaining four times.

At our first appointment together we had a fight. A repeat fight. Jason had been to visit me one time, last year, in LA, soon after he'd broken up with his girlfriend and months before I'd gone to Medjugorje. We went to see *Austin Powers* and were the first to arrive at the theater at noontime. We stood in the lobby, off to the side so I could lean on the closed concession stand. A small crowd of people began to arrive and to form a line at the center of the lobby in front of the theater door, behavior I deemed predictable and regimented.

When the doors opened, I headed to the front of the line, and Jason had a hissy fit: "You are so rude." He hung back so I was forced to rejoin him. "You can't just go to the front of the line."

"We were here first."

"But they made a line. You can't just barge in front."

"That's their problem if they think they have to form a line. I don't form lines. I was here first."

"You are unbelievable—unbelievable! So self-centered. I can't even believe you."

I was enraged at his judging me. My son was a stickler for rules, and I hated rules. How did the two of us get stuck with each other? Somewhere at the edge of my mind I'd known I should put a lid on my fury, but couldn't. I knew my anger came from the resentment I felt for having been held back by Jason from doing what I'd wanted when I was young. At the center of his feelings was resentment for having a mother who didn't consider his wants or his feelings nearly enough.

And then in therapy, after all my praying, all my regret, a river of tears, I could not control my anger when Jason used the *Austin Powers* incident to illustrate how inconsiderate I was.

"They formed the line. It was *their* problem." I could feel my face clench.

"Beverly?" the therapist said. "I think Jason just wants you to act like a mother."

"Act like a mother." That caught me up short. What did she mean? Not defend myself? Acquiesce even though I know he is wrong? What was the matter with me? Here I was, praying to beat the band, drenched in religion, crying my heart out morning, noon, and night. I'm in conversation with my son, who I'd thought had deserted me for good, and I'm still unable to contain my rage. Would I never grow up?

Later, alone at my friend Kirsten's apartment, I calmed down enough to understand what our therapist meant by saying, "Jason wants you to act like a mother." Jason needed me to acknowledge his point of view, his needs, and not be defensive, not argue, and not insist that he respect my needs too, at least not in that moment. I felt ashamed of myself. Would Mary be ashamed of me, too? No. No, Mary would know how hard I am trying. Mary would be patient with me. And so would I.

Before Jason's and my next appointment together, I went to mass on Sunday at a church that had been recommended on the Upper East Side. The first thing I noticed was a Pietà, and I wondered if I'd been led to this of all churches because there was something to learn from the visage of Mary with her adult son draped over her lap. I knelt in front of Mary and was reminded of how my son's pain makes me so uncomfortable I want to run from it, because I can't fix it. I feel powerless to help, and it's all made more intense by the fact that I, his mother, am the cause of so much of his hurting. Mary had stood and watched her son die in agony, and looking at Mary now, holding her grown son as he's slipped down to her from the cross, I understood something so simple yet profound. I didn't have to try to fix anything. All I had to do was listen—feel his pain—acknowledge his truth, tell him I'm sorry, and comfort him.

Jason needed to be reminded of how young I was, how unformed, how disappointed in life, at the time he was born. He'd never heal until he could forgive me.

But most importantly of all, Jason needed my compassion. I'd learned from Mary that compassion is feeling the other person's hurt. I'd been running from the truth, too ashamed to hear from Jason's mouth what I'd done to him. I hadn't asked the question "How did you feel when . . . ?" because I was terrified of feeling the pain I'd inflicted on my son.

During our next therapy session, Jason told me that it had been a blow when I'd moved to LA. I'd given him a home to bring his friends to in Orient and then I'd pulled up and moved. "Did you ever think of how I would feel?" he asked me.

I had, but not really.

"I thought the distance would be good," I told him. "That we were too close, that we needed to separate." I think, too, I was afraid of my attachment to him, of my need, of my deep love feelings. I'd been afraid to be intimate with my child.

"Too close?" He was incredulous.

"Would you like to be closer now?"

He nodded.

"You would like it if I called you up, like once a week?"

"Well . . . I . . ."

"If you want to be close . . ."

"Yeah. I'd like you to call once a week."

"It's a two-way street. You can call, too."

"I know."

It *is* a two-way street. But I'm his mother. I can give more.

Afterwards, Jason and I went to lunch to an Italian restaurant around the block from our old apartment. The sunlight lit the white tablecloth, and the fabric felt warm under my hand. "Nice," I said to Jase, fanning my hand across the table in the light.

"Huh?"

"The sun." There was something on his mind. I should ask him what it was; he was going to tell me something that would hurt. My ribs clutched my heart, a wall—no, a cell—of protection. I used to think my heart was safe there, but it was just walled in.

The waiter took our order. I ordered a risotto, Jason a pasta; we'd share.

After the waiter poured our water and walked away, I felt dizzy. I was about to ask, and Jason was about to answer me true. The truth would hurt, but it would also heal.

"What are you thinking about?"

"I never trusted you after that night."

I knew exactly what night.

It was two weeks before I had finally left Nigel.

Before that night it had been different. I'd been Jason's protector. I'd even been his hero sometimes. I knew because I'd seen it in Jason's eyes. One Christmas on our way to Connecticut, we were waiting for the number 6 train at the Spring Street station. Jason was ten and staring down the track, hoping to spot the lights of the approaching train. I was sitting on a bench. Out of nowhere, a drunken man in a sport jacket and tie lunged for Jason, his hands on my son's shoulders. I leaped for the man, grabbed his coat collar and pulled him, then pushed him in the chest, sending him flying back as I roared from deep in my belly, "Get your fucking hands off of my son!"

When I linked arms with Jason back on the bench, he said, "Wow, Ma! You were strong."

A year later, Jason and I were in the elevator after seeing a movie with Nigel. Jason had loved the movie, and when Nigel said something witty, making fun of it, Jason said under his breath, "What do you know? Idiot."

Nigel reared up, raising his hand. I pulled Jason behind me and yelled, "Don't you ever raise your hand to my son— ever! I'll murder you!"

When the elevator doors opened, I grabbed Jason's hand and pulled him along with me and away from Nigel. There was a trippy lightness in Jason's step. "We're leaving him?" he asked.

"Yes."

We slept on my friend Tracy's floor that night. In the dark Jason's face turned toward mine on the pillow we shared. "You never would let him hit me, would you, Ma," he stated instead of asked.

"I will never let anyone touch you."

We stayed at Tracy's a few nights while I looked for a job. Nigel called six times a day, apologizing, begging forgiveness, begging me to come home. This was before things went so wrong with us, and so I went back.

Now, in the restaurant, Jason said, "You hid by my bed."

This night had been lurking, unspoken, between Jason and me. I'd known in my heart but did not want to remember that night or acknowledge what I'd done to my son.

It was near the end of our nightmare with Nigel, and Nigel had found a letter addressed to "My Friends" that I'd written and hadn't sent. I tried to explain why none of them had heard from me for so long: "Did you ever hide when you hear a knock on the door? Did you ever take a drink after breakfast because you can't stand your own face in the mirror? Did you ever fantasize dropping a brick on your lover's head? I do. . . ."

Nigel flew into a rage. He stomped back and forth in front of me and pulled his hair. He hugged himself and trembled, sobbing. When I tried to make light of his rage by offering to buy cigarettes, he blocked the door and pushed me down. A short while later, when he left to get beers next door, I ran up the stairs and hid between Jason's bed and the wall. "Don't let Nigel know I'm here," I'd whispered.

I'd used the one person in the world it was my responsibility to protect—to protect me.

"I'm so sorry, Jase." I placed my hand on top of his and felt the pain of the little lost boy I didn't love enough, the boy I didn't take care of well, the pain of the grown man whose hand I was holding across the table—and it didn't kill me.

I knew Jason would have to forgive me before his anger would melt. I wished I could help him to get there, even as I knew in a visceral way, for the first time, that my guilt would do my son no good at all.

I could feel sorry for the pain I inflicted, but I would also have compassion for myself. The mistakes I'd made, the bad relationships, the drunkenness were the growing pains of a confused young woman; I'd been a mother at the same time I was growing up. The only real tragedy was that my child had been hurt by it.

I was not an evil person. I truly had done the best I could. And like Jason's father, I'd been incapable.

That Jason was born to a girl who did not want to be a mother was his cross to bear. I can love him, I can feel sorry for the past, I can regret the mother I was not till my dying breath, but Jason will have to find his own way.

In bed that night I thanked Mary for giving me the courage I needed to be a mother.

I decided I had to go back to San Miguel to witness its Easter celebration, which is renowned all over Mexico. On the Thursday night before Easter all the statues are taken down and decorations are put up in their place, like an art installation. One church had little girls with wings and halos holding wands up on the altar, which had been festooned with thousands of flowers. On Good Friday, I sat on a curb watching intently as the familiar statues that had been removed from the churches the night before were marched through the streets, their garments rippling in the breeze, their bodies swaying as if they were alive. The procession began with Christ in agony on his cross, followed by a truly scary, flesh-and-blood, ham-fisted Pilate leading his legion of Roman soldiers, all white men with whips and a bristle of brush on the top of their helmets. Their sandaled feet took a step after every third ominous beat of the drum. The army was followed by hundreds of beautiful Mexican girl *angelitas,* dressed in communion white. Then magnificent angel statues riding on flower-covered pallets held aloft by stately women dressed in black. Each angel held something significant: three nails, a crown, Christ's clothes, a replica of the Shroud of Turin. The rooster that crowed three times had his own pallet. There were an orchestra, a men's chorus, and a children's chorus, and then there was Christ in his coffin, followed by Mary weeping, her black train stretching half a block, and lastly Mary Magdalene, whom the Bible says Christ "kissed on the mouth." (Did this mean they were lovers? I hoped so.) By the time the procession was over I felt like I'd witnessed the real thing. I'd sat amid the Mexicans, all of us crowded onto the sidewalk and into the gutter. Children were passed around from mother to father to older siblings. They ate ice creams, they sucked on lollipop rings. They made friendly eyes at me. I made friendly eyes at them and was reminded of my visit to a day-care center with my friend Juliet a few weeks before. Juliet is Mexican and something of a "teacher." She read my astrological chart and told me I needed to practice love. I said, "How do I do that?"

She said, "By holding babies."

Funny she should say that, because I'd tried to volunteer to hold crack babies back in LA, but when I couldn't find a hospital with such a program after two tries, I gave up.

Life is more direct, and visceral, in Mexico. Juliet and I went to the clinic that helps teenage mothers. The woman at the desk said regretfully that we'd just missed two babies who were sent home, and right at this moment there was a baby being born, but that could take some time. A baby was being born behind the closed door in front of us right at this moment? A new baby would be handed to a teenage girl? A new baby would be put in her young arms? Their lives would begin together? Her life would forever be changed? A lump formed in my throat, and I insisted to Juliet that we sit on the bench and wait. And we did for a while; but Juliet had only an hour more, so she suggested we drive to the other side of town where the clinic also has a day-care center for the babies of the teenage mothers.

There were six babies. A boy who crawled like a bat out of hell and was not interested in us. Another little boy in suspenders, skinny as a spider, a nose that needed to be wiped. But when I saw the little girl, I knew what Juliet meant about practicing love. She was so tiny standing in her crib, silently weeping. She held her arms out to me, but then when I came near, she shook her head no, still crying. *"Donde está tu mamá?"* Where is your mother? I asked her.

The little girl held up her arm limply and pointed. *"Alla,"* she said with such loneliness, such longing. *"Alla."* Somewhere.

But not here. I knew the frightened, homesick feeling. We all felt it as kids; and as adults alone in the night, looking at our own reflections in the window of a moving train, we feel it still. It's the feeling of being separated from God. I wanted badly to pull that child to my chest, let her feel my heartbeat, my warmth, to comfort her, but she wouldn't have it. Only her mother could comfort her. As only I could comfort Jason. And as only Mary could have comforted me.

I was scheduled to leave Mexico at the crack of dawn on Monday. It was Friday. The alarm went off. I opened my eyes and knew one thing: I did not want to leave. Life was softer in Mexico; it was a feminine country with a mother

God. I would have liked to live in a place where "why" and "because" sound like the same word. But I had to leave, and I had a million things to attend to before I did. It was seven-thirty. I showered and dressed and put on my watch, which said it was ten-thirty. Impossible. It had stopped in the night, and now, in addition to everything else I had to do, I'd have to take it to the shop where I'd bought it the previous week. It was just as well. I'd been meaning to get to La Salud and pay my respects to Niño Santo and Dolorosa before I left, and this was my chance—the clock shop was across the square from the church.

I ran around doing errands, then began my daily rosary on my fingers as I walked the cobblestone streets to La Salud, where I sat in front of El Niño and Dolorosa and closed my eyes. "Show me your will," I said, then, "Let me see with eyes of love," and began my twenty-minute meditation. I tried to make time every day to think about God, to sit and to listen, as well as to say my rosary. Faith took work, but it was easier in Mexico, where they say, *"Con fe se tiene todo."* With faith you have everything.

Faith is beyond reason, and in Mexico logic is not at a premium; in fact, it's sometimes hard to find. Mexicans believe every leaf has its own spirit; they give their dead a feast once a year, where they cook the dead persons' favorite foods, buy their favorite cigarettes, pour glasses of booze. The worst thing you can do is ask in a store for something that has run out. If others have asked too, the shopkeeper may not reorder it, because the item had caused disappointment, and trouble.

At La Salud I crossed myself, said goodbye to the Niño, and

touched Dolorosa's skirt, then gave five pesos to the beggar woman at the door. I walked across the road to the watch shop, and as the woman took my watch, then looked at her own, I noticed it *was* ten-thirty, and my watch began ticking. The woman removed the battery and tested it. It was fine.

Surely, the stopped watch had been a sign from Mary, a way to get me to go to church and to pay attention. And so I spent my last days in Mexico with a heightened awareness of the divine, and on the lookout for signs.

Later in the afternoon, I met my friend Karen, who'd moved to Mexico nine years ago, the same time Kip and I had moved away. Karen knew of a studio apartment for rent. It was only two hundred dollars, which meant I could afford to rent it and still keep my place in LA. I wanted to secure a foothold in Mexico to ensure that I'd always return and stay tapped into the divine. But after looking at the place, I decided it was too small to be comfortable and I didn't want it. As Karen and I sat in her Volkswagen, she said, "What is your plan, anyway?"

"Well," I said. "I have to find out what my next gig is, and if I don't have to be in the States to write it, I'll move down here."

"That's not how it works," Karen said. "You have to move here on faith, then you'll find a way."

I felt as though she'd thrown down the gauntlet.

That night Juliet and I sat on a veranda on a hill overlooking the village, and she told me how she'd just taken her German nephew, a medical student, to the desert and picked him some peyote. In the summer while I was here, Juliet had a Huichol shaman sleeping in her backyard whose teacher was peyote. He ran a feather wand over me and sucked three little rocks from my body—black from my heart, clear from my throat, and white from my brain. The shaman held them in the palm of his hand and told me that someone had cast a spell on me. The spell might have been tossed at me on the street, but it also might have been cast long ago, which would be more serious. The shaman told me to pay attention to my dreams. If I dreamed of bananas on trees, tomato plants, corn in the fields, then I would know that my dreams could come true. But if I dreamed of darkness and death, I must come back and see him again. Juliet, who was translating, said that those images were the shaman's images for abundance and that my images might be different. That night I dreamed of fields of gold with Frank Sinatra singing in the breeze.

Now, on the veranda, sipping sangria, I told Juliet about my watch stopping and my being coerced into visiting church; then I told her what Karen had said.

"I didn't know how I would say this," Juliet said, "but I was going to tell you the same thing. This is your life. When you feel a call to do something, you must do it."

Her words had the ring of truth; Mary might even be speaking through her. "I have to find a place before I leave!" I fairly shouted.

That night I called Jason. "Would you mind if I moved to Mexico?"

"You kidding? I love Mexico."

I could hardly sleep for the planning of my move. I'd have to return to LA to pack up, then visit my family and friends back east. It was April. I figured it was safe to plan on arriving in Mexico by July 1. Maybe I could rent a place in San Miguel immediately and leave it empty if I needed to. As I tossed in bed, I thought of an anecdote Karen had told me about her daughter, Ida, who is nine and precocious, and her husband, who is a painter. They'd just returned from Oaxaca, where they'd gone for Easter with another family. The boy of the other family was twelve and tortured Ida the whole drive there. In the motel room at night Ida said to her mother and father, "I wish Richard would just shut up. I know there's no such thing as the Easter Bunny. But it's good to use your imagination."

Karen's husband said, "I believe in the Easter Bunny."

And I believed in God. I do not mean to make light of my hard-won new faith, but sometimes it just plain felt good, like being a kid and believing in the Easter Bunny; it felt right to accept mystery, and forces beyond our senses, and to believe in miracles.

I got up for the third time to refill my glass with water, and after I drank half of it, I finally fell asleep.

The next morning I was determined to go to every bulletin board and call every number advertising an apartment. My only criterion was that there be two bedrooms, so Jason would know he had a room of his own in my house. There were two or three possibilities at the first board, and the second place I stopped was Chelo's pharmacy. Chelo had been widowed four times. When Juliet told me this about Chelo one night at dinner, she'd said, "What I want to know is how she got the fourth one to marry her. I bet she went to the Sonora market and got the herb that takes away the will of a man." I was thinking I could go to the Sonora market, take peyote in the desert, visit the town I'd heard of where balls of light are seen bouncing around the mountain on Good Friday.

And then my heart did a cha-cha as I remembered how I'd been invited to paint icons with a woman named Mary Jane the week before. Mary Jane paints icons as a form of prayer, a meditation in which you commune with the saint you are painting, and you must try to paint the icon you are copying exactly the same, but every icon turns out different. Mary Jane had told me she loved Jesus but had thrown out fifteen Bibles. When we looked in the index of her latest Bible for "Virgin Mary" and there was no listing, she threw that one away, too.

If I lived here, I could continue my inspired yoga classes, at which the other morning I had done the impossible by actually placing my foot behind my head, and as we lay down at the end of the class, the teacher had read this quote from Dharma:

> *The thought manifests as the word*
> *The word manifests as the deed*
> *The deed develops into habit*
> *And the habit hardens into character.*
> *So watch the thought*
> *And its ways with care*
> *And let it spring from love*
> *Born out of respect for all beings.*

Chelo the pharmacist, who is a slight, shy woman with dreamy skin and a easy smile, had just opened up. I'd heard that she was rich in real estate, which she'd inherited from her four dead husbands, and so I asked her if she had or knew of anything for rent.

The house is on Loreto Street, named after Mary's house, flown by the angels from Nazareth. It's around the corner from the church of Niño Santo, whose dome I can almost touch from my rooftop. I am moving there in July.

From Mexico I had sent Jason a card of the Virgin of Guadalupe, which Jason had assured me he'd stuck to his refrigerator with the Virgin of Guadalupe magnets I'd also sent him. I was afraid I might be guilty of overkill, until Jason e-mailed me in Mexico asking me to send him a silver chain so he could wear his Medjugorje medal. My greatest hope is that Our Lady has answered my prayers and is sneaking into my son's heart, too, the way she sneaked into mine.

Back home in LA before I moved to Mexico, I went to church on Mother's Day. But because I didn't want to miss a special chanting session at my yoga studio, I couldn't make it to Saint Augustine's in time for their last morning mass and so had gone to Saint Monica's, which was the church closest to my house. The congregation at Saint Monica's is very white and upper-middle-class, which I like to avoid, and the priests have a smug, self-satisfied air, because, I assume, they have filled their pews, thanks mostly to their music ministry—a veritable orchestra with a conductor up at the altar. And I was particularly annoyed because it was

Mother's Day, and although the youngish, rosy-cheeked priest did manage to slip in a cute little anecdote about his own mother, Mother Mary was never mentioned—not once. I had been to only one mass in the United States where a Hail Mary was said at all. And last Christmas, I heard about how strong Joseph's faith was for listening to the angel in his dream, yet Mary and her faith were not mentioned at all.

But Mary's statue was right up there next to the altar, everyone in the congregation prays the Hail Mary at home, and I was sick to death of the patriarchal American Church's blatant dismissal of the Mother of God, while it was Mary who'd probably brought half of us to these pews and kept us here.

I was so annoyed, I went through one of my little church fits, in which I have to exert superhuman will to keep my bottom in the seat. This time, though, it didn't work, and as the priest turned from the lectern, I stood to leave. But then the beginning strains of "Ave Maria" filled the air, goose bumps tickled every inch of my skin, and I sat back down.

Maybe it was good the Catholic Church didn't often bring Mary up in church; it left her out of the trinity and kept her in mystery.

After "Ave Maria," the priest stood at the top of the aisle and invited all the mothers to come up for a blessing. I thought, I'm not going up, it's too hokey. What about the women in the church who wanted to be mothers but couldn't? This was discriminatory. What about my friends whose deepest grief in life is that they didn't have a baby when they were young enough, and now it's too late? Or my friends who never found a decent man? But then, as I watched a very old lady file out of her pew, humbly smiling, and wearing a pink carnation, I thought, But I'm a mother. I would *like* to be honored.

And so I stood with all the mothers, and as my eyes filled with church tears, I thought, I have to thank Jason for this.

When I got home, there were four messages from my son; he'd been trying to wish me a happy Mother's Day.

When I called him back, I said, "Jase, I had a revelation at church this morning. I want to thank you for making me be a mother."

"You're welcome," he said. "It's about time."

A PENGUIN READERS GUIDE TO

LOOKING
FOR
MARY

Beverly Donofrio

Looking for Mary
READING GROUP DISCUSSION GUIDE

As Beverly Donofrio approached midlife, she found herself
caught between two poles: She was both searching for someone to
love her unconditionally, the way a mother would, and trying to
learn how to be a better mother to her grown son, Jason. Pregnant
at seventeen, divorced by nineteen, Donofrio was determined, with
her young son in tow, to live life on her own terms—first as a
college student and later as an aspiring writer in New York City.

But by the time she is forty, a crack appears in her tough façade.
While shopping at a yard sale, Donofrio is captivated by the sight
of an old, framed postcard of the Virgin Mary. She buys it; as time
passes, she buys several more, and soon images of the Virgin Mary
are decorating nearly every wall of her house. At first, Donofrio
convinces herself that she is collecting the images merely for their
kitsch value. "Mary's image on my wall was a joke," she writes, "an
iconic ideal of a mother I could never be, the type of mother I
scoffed at: a passive, sexless, adoring—or weeping, wounded, and
suffering—mama."

But her "kitschy" collection gradually becomes a shrine, and, in
Donofrio's words, "knowing a good opportunity when she sees one,
the Blessed Mother came in." A few years later, citing her
professional curiosity as a writer, Donofrio embarks on a pilgrimage
to the Bosnian holy city of Medjugorje, where the Virgin Mary
has been appearing to villagers and pilgrims since 1984. She
participates in a ten-day fasting retreat along with a group of
devoted Catholics from the United States. At first, she observes her
fellow pilgrims warily, with the detached air of a non-believer, a
journalist who is there simply to do her job. But soon, like the

Mary paintings and framed postcards that fill her home, the miracles she witnesses begin to fill her heart.

Donofrio weaves stories of her young adulthood in New York with scenes from her Bosnian retreat. In one moment, she is in Medjugorje, standing with a group of overweight suburbanites, sharing in the miracle of a spinning sun; then, she is hiding behind her son's bed in a loft in New York City, hoping her drunken artist lover won't find her. These flashback scenes are recounted with unflinching honesty, and her recklessness as a mother is stunning. (Years later, Jason tells her "I never felt safe with you," and the words continue to haunt her.)

While Donofrio once scoffed at the image of a weeping, wounded and suffering mama, years later she became that image: weeping and prostrate, sorrowful for the son she wasn't able to properly love. She wonders if "pain, terrible need, is the only path to God." A search for the relief from heartbreak may have been the catalyst for Donofrio's journey, but in the end, it doesn't really matter how she came to love the Virgin Mary and reaffirm her faith. Ultimately, she asserts, what matters most is not how she arrived at her faith, but that she has reached it at all. "It's like night and day, the way I felt before and the way I feel now," she writes. Donofrio may have spent the better part of a decade looking for Mary, but in the end, she seems to have found what she was looking for all along: herself.

INTERVIEW WITH BEVERLY DONOFRIO

1. You write that you "would have fallen off your chair laughing" if anyone had told you that in the future you'd be at a religious retreat praying the rosary. Have friends or acquaintances found it hard to accept your transformation?

I think my friends and my family are happy for me and have adopted a "whatever turns you on—as long as you don't try to convince me" attitude. I take this to heart and do not proselytize, but I also don't censor myself. I'm a storyteller and so I continue to tell my stories, which are now often about some insight or illumination that has to do with God or faith, because that's what most interests me. I recently told some friends about how I'd been stuck in New York City on business for nearly two months and began going to church everyday as an antidote to all the noise and frenzy. It was around the time that *Looking for Mary* had come out and a film-maker wanted to interview me for a piece to be published in an arty downtown magazine. He told me that even though the book was about the Virgin Mary, he didn't think the article would be a hard sell because "You're one of us." I was taken aback by that statement for a moment, and it must have showed because the filmmaker explained, "You're an artist. You struggled downtown in the East Village for years." I felt so far away from that time but didn't say so.

The next day I went to noon mass, as usual, with the fifty or so middle-aged to old ladies and, maybe, a half-dozen men. We were of different races and classes, and the lady who gave the readings reminded me of my mother. I sat in my regular spot, happy to be there, but this time after communion, instead of closing my eyes and praying, I watched the other people as they turned from the altar—Christ on their tongues, faith in their hearts—and realized:

These are my people. This thought filled me with humility as tears of relief streamed down my face.

I didn't tell that story to everyone I know, but I told it to my closest friends and they seemed to understand how I'd felt.

2. Since "Mary knows a good opportunity when she sees one," do you think Mary chose you as a messenger? Do you hope that your book inspires others to embark on their own spiritual journeys?

I do think Mary chose me to be a messenger. I think Mary chooses many people to be her messengers. My message happened to be more public than most because I'm a memoirist, a fact which, of course, Mary knew and used. I believe the woman is one of the most gifted self-promoters on the planet: Her portrait has been painted more often than probably anyone's; she tirelessly makes personal appearances—over two hundred in the twentieth century alone, and now I've written this book about her, a drop in the bucket.

I would be disappointed if my book did not lead at least a few people to a spiritual path, which does not, by the way, need to be the same spiritual path I have chosen.

3. How do you regard all of your Mary memorabilia now? Are they holy objects or kitsch?

I have never thought of my Mary collection as holy objects. To the extent that they make me think of Mary or give me comfort when I gaze at them, they are invaluable to me. Some pieces in my collection might be regarded as kitsch, because they are painted with glitter, for example, or have a colored light bulb within the frame, but they are absolutely beautiful and precious to me, kitsch or no kitsch.

4. In addition to sharing the story of your conversion, the book also reads like a love letter to your son. Did you make a conscious decision to write this book in the hope that it would help Jason come to a deeper understanding about you and the decisions you've made in your life? Has your relationship with him changed since the publication of your book?

I did not make a conscious decision to write this book hoping my son would understand me, my life, or the things I have done. I wrote the book because I write about my life and I recognized this spiritual call as one of the most important things that had ever happened to me. I knew that I had to ask forgiveness from God. I hoped that if I could believe God forgave me then I would be able to forgive myself. I, of course, hoped Jason would forgive me, too, for selfish reasons, sure, but mostly because I knew that anger and resentment would be poison to hold onto.

One night before the book was published but after it had been accepted and basically sent down the editing chute, I received a phone call from Jason. He told me he loved me and forgave me and wanted to be close again, the way we used to be. It's what I'd been praying to Mary for for a couple of years. Jase and I both wept. Jason has now graduated from therapy, is off anti-depressants, and is getting married this summer to a wonderful woman. For all of this, I thank Mary.

5. You write about your disdain for the patriarchal church and male-only priests of Catholicism. Do you intend this to be a feminist book?

I did not consciously set out to write a feminist book. I am, however, a feminist, so any book I write will be inherently feminist whether I intend it or not.

6. The places you have lived—New York, Orient, Mexico—play a large role in the book. You write that in Orient you were happy; when you moved to New York, you were miserable and ended up checking yourself into a psychiatric clinic. How has location played a role in your life? Do you blame New York itself or was it just the unwitting backdrop of a difficult period?

I think, for many people, the time they graduate from college is difficult and frightening. It's hard to get your foot in the door, to find a way to begin your chosen profession. I was filled with self-doubts about whether I was gifted with the talent to be a writer, and now was the time that I would find out. My coming-of-age was made more difficult by moving to New York with no money and a ten-year-old son in tow. The city made absolutely nothing—professionally or personally—easier. So, I guess I do blame New York for at least some of the difficulty I experienced back then.

I know something about myself I did not know then: I need fresh air, silence, bird song, the patter of rain on a roof, the whisper of wind, sun on the top of my head, big skies, blankets of stars, and great vistas of open spaces—in other words, nature. It's so much easier for me to feel the presence of God there.

7. At the close of the book, you are preparing to move to Mexico, where Mary has a huge presence in the consciousness of the general population. How has your belief in Mary evolved since finishing this book and moving to Mexico?

I don't know that my belief in Mary has evolved or changed. I do know that I don't have to look very far to find her—she's a daily presence in my life—and I also know that at least for me it helps to be constantly reminded of her by running into her image every time I turn around. She's in fountains, on the tops of walls. She stands on corners, she's glued to people's car windows. It's common to run into a pilgrimage on a highway or a side road and see the Virgin in one of her miraculous incarnations tied to car and truck hoods, harnessed to the backs of cyclists, carried on pallets by walkers. Every time I witness this, I flush with goosebumps and I want to yell, "you go, Girl!"

8. What are you working on now? Does Mary figure in your next book?

I am just beginning a historical novel set in Orient in the mid-1800s. I don't know yet if Mary will figure in it, but God certainly does. I am also writing, as I always have, a collection of slices of life, incidents, insights, stories of things that happen to me and to other people, some of which will make their way into a third memoir—and so will Mary, I have no doubt.

QUESTIONS FOR DISCUSSION

1. What role do women play in the book, as mentors and friends to the author? How are their roles different from that of men?

2. Do you think Donofrio was essentially a good mother to Jason? What do you think about her attempts to earn her son's forgiveness?

3. Do you think the story would have been different if Donofrio had had a daughter instead of a son? Would she have made the same lifestyle choices? How would another female character affect the structure and themes of the story?

4. When Donofrio is living in Orient, she invites a psychiatrist to her home, whom she overhears asking another guest, "What do you think of Beverly's Mary cathexis?" Do you think there is a psychological reason for her deeply felt identification with Mary? Is it fair, or even useful, to bring a modern, psychological reading to a person's religious beliefs?

5. Although she downplays its significance, what do you make of Donofrio's comment that her mother's Mary sighting as a child "had probably planted the seed for my search for Mary"?

6. Donofrio claims that the Mexican people love and worship Mary with a fervor equal to that of their love for Jesus, noting that churchgoers in the United States don't seem to be able to match that level of adoration for the Blessed Virgin. Does this say anything about the differences between the two cultures?

7. How large a role does Medjugorje play in the book? What did you find more interesting: the passages that take place in Bosnia or those on Donofrio's young adulthood? Why?

8. Donofrio writes that she "suffered deeply, and it was only then, in my desperation, that I was able to let Mary in." What does the search for relief from suffering say about a person's motives for finding faith? Is a person more devout if he or she worships unconditionally, without hoping for a payoff?

For additional copies of this guide, or for more information about other Penguin Readers Guides, please call the Penguin Marketing Department at (800) 778-6425, e-mail us at reading@penguinputnam.com, or write to us at:

Penguin Books Marketing Dept. CC
Readers Guides, 375 Hudson Street
New York, NY 10014-3657

Please allow 4–6 weeks for delivery
To access Penguin Readers Guides online, visit the PPI Web site at www.penguinputnam.com

FOR THE BEST IN PAPERBACKS, LOOK FOR THE Ⓟ

In every corner of the world, on every subject under the sun, Penguin represents quality and variety—the very best in publishing today.

For complete information about books available from Penguin—including Penguin Classics, Penguin Compass, and Puffins—and how to order them, write to us at the appropriate address below. Please note that for copyright reasons the selection of books varies from country to country.

In the United States: Please write to *Penguin Group (USA), P.O. Box 12289 Dept. B, Newark, New Jersey 07101-5289* or call 1-800-788-6262.

In the United Kingdom: Please write to *Dept. EP, Penguin Books Ltd, Bath Road, Harmondsworth, West Drayton, Middlesex UB7 0DA.*

In Canada: Please write to *Penguin Books Canada Ltd, 10 Alcorn Avenue, Suite 300, Toronto, Ontario M4V 3B2.*

In Australia: Please write to *Penguin Books Australia Ltd, P.O. Box 257, Ringwood, Victoria 3134.*

In New Zealand: Please write to *Penguin Books (NZ) Ltd, Private Bag 102902, North Shore Mail Centre, Auckland 10.*

In India: Please write to *Penguin Books India Pvt Ltd, 11 Panchsheel Shopping Centre, Panchsheel Park, New Delhi 110 017.*

In the Netherlands: Please write to *Penguin Books Netherlands bv, Postbus 3507, NL-1001 AH Amsterdam.*

In Germany: Please write to *Penguin Books Deutschland GmbH, Metzlerstrasse 26, 60594 Frankfurt am Main.*

In Spain: Please write to *Penguin Books S. A., Bravo Murillo 19, 1° B, 28015 Madrid.*

In Italy: Please write to *Penguin Italia s.r.l., Via Benedetto Croce 2, 20094 Corsico, Milano.*

In France: Please write to *Penguin France, Le Carré Wilson, 62 rue Benjamin Baillaud, 31500 Toulouse.*

In Japan: Please write to *Penguin Books Japan Ltd, Kaneko Building, 2-3-25 Koraku, Bunkyo-Ku, Tokyo 112.*

In South Africa: Please write to *Penguin Books South Africa (Pty) Ltd, Private Bag X14, Parkview, 2122 Johannesburg.*